"The Stories the Stones Might Tell"
The Chambers Family's Rock Ledge Ranch, 1874-1900

D1708098

Elizabeth Marshall Borders

2022

2

For all my Rock Ledge Ranch family,
who have made the Chambers' story come alive,
but especially for Mrs. Donna Tomaselli,
who wanted it all written down with sources properly cited.

Table of Contents

Introduction

Making History

Somewhere within the walls of the Rock Ledge House in the year 1885, Elsie Woolsey Chambers wrote a story. More than a story, a history. Pondering the removal of the original cabin on the Rock Ledge Ranch property, Elsie W. Chambers sat down with pencil and paper to write an account she titled "What Happened While the Cabin Lived." Elsie and her husband Robert had left this cabin on their land for several years after they bought the ranch in 1874 before they eventually tore it down. Not wanting it to be lost for good, Elsie chronicled the cabin's brief history. The story, however, is not really about the cabin. Rather than dwelling on the ranch's first occupant, Walter Galloway, and what happened within his cabin, Elsie used the cabin as a framework for the history of what happened outside it. Her account chronicles the events experienced by the first wave of settlers who had been making history in the Colorado Springs area. Although the Chambers removed the cabin, they preserved its memories. Perceptively, Elsie envisioned that the story of Walter Galloway and his property could be used as a window into the larger themes and history of the period. Their land had value beyond its borders. Their story could tell a broader story about their community, region, state, and even their country.

This is the basic premise of microhistory. Microhistory perceives the unique ability of individual stories to reveal larger themes and ideas. It seeks to learn about the universals through the particulars. One can understand the common man by looking at an individual man, the daily struggle by seeing what one person faced in a day, the victories of a period by examining one family's success. To engage in microhistory is to search for the truth in the stories of everyday people, places, objects, and actions. How did people handle difficult circumstances? What did people really think and feel? What changed their lives? Individual stories can reveal elements of the past that historians would otherwise miss. Houses and homes of the past hold stories that textbooks, museums, and battlefields cannot.

Elsie W. Chambers recognized this. Looking back across the previous decades of history in the Pikes Peak region, she realized that Galloway's cabin provided a means to explore that story. Her life in the town of Colorado Springs was possible because of those first settlers. Gratefully, she set out to record the improvements they had brought. As a pioneer who, with her family, had worked to bring growth to this western town, she noted the importance of remembering what made settlement in the region possible. She sought to leave a description of what pioneers had done, what they were doing, and what they could do in the future. If her children and grandchildren knew this story of what had come before, they could accomplish greater things still. In "What Happened While the Cabin Lived," Elsie W. Chambers used one humble dwelling to tell a broader story beyond those four wooden walls.

This book presents a continuation of the Chambers' legacy. If the small Galloway homestead cabin can teach about the early history of the Colorado Springs region, how much more can the Rock Ledge House contribute! Elsie W. Chambers, her husband Robert, and their three children Benjamin, Eleanor, and Mary left behind more evidence than the first homesteader did. A whole house, for one thing! Beyond that, photographs, newspaper advertisements, tax records, and other primary documents reveal details about the twenty-five years they spent at the Ranch. Yet can this house, these people, and these documents chronicle more than just the Chambers family's story? Can their home, like the cabin, tell the story of the region, the state, and the West? The history of the Chambers family's life at Rock Ledge Ranch between 1874 and 1900 describes the development of Colorado Springs as a home for invalids, an agricultural battlefield, and an anti-frontier town.[1] The Chambers were both exemplary and essential in their community, so the major themes of their lives reflect important themes in the Colorado Springs region.

Understanding the context for the Colorado Springs in which the Chambers arrived, however, is a necessary first step. Chapter One seeks to do this by recounting the early history of exploration and settlement in Colorado. What drew individuals to Colorado? What kept them there? Who lived here before their arrival? What made Colorado Springs an attractive home? How developed was it when they arrived? This first chapter establishes the state of the Colorado territory when the Chambers disembarked from the train in 1874.

Motivations for immigration are an important part of any pioneer's story, and no less so for the Chambers. Chapter Two explores the Chambers' motives for their move to Colorado. Furthermore, it explores how that same motivation in other immigrants constituted an important source of income for the Chambers. Like many others, the Chambers were drawn from Pennsylvania to Colorado because of health concerns. Would the climate cure work? If it did, could they make a living? In short, health-seeking brought the family to Colorado Springs—and helped keep them there.

Yet survival out West required multiple incomes in order to weather the many obstacles present in the nineteenth century. Furthermore, the Chambers bought a significant parcel of property with water rights for a reason: they wanted to continue farming. Chapter Three gets into the weeds of the many challenges the Chambers faced as farmers in Colorado. It shows how they overcame everything that the climate, the locusts, and the law could throw at them. They faced the same

---

[1] This term "anti-frontier town" was coined by historian David Hamer and used by historian Gregory Atkins in his article "'Business Sense if Not Souls:' Boosters and Religion in Colorado Springs, 1871-1909." An anti-frontier town could be defined as one where "strong companies or founders directed growth and sought to rid or reduce negative frontier stereotypes." In many cases, this meant discouraging the saloon and alcohol while encouraging church and other religious organizations. Gregory Atkins, "'Business Sense if Not Souls:' Boosters and Religion in Colorado Springs, 1871-1909," (*The Journal of the Gilded Age and Progressive Era* 17, no. 1, 2018), 79.

obstacles as most Colorado farmers, but by working with their neighbors, diversifying their agricultural efforts, and persevering in innovation, the Chambers reaped success in their agricultural efforts.

Though they certainly had enough work on the ranch to keep them busy, the Chambers were not focused merely on survival. Chapter Four details their involvement in the city through church, school, and other community organizations that were essential to the development of Colorado Springs. Seeking to throw off stereotypes of the rugged and wild West, Colorado Springs founders instead planned and built a community that would resemble towns back East. This would not be a boom-and-bust town. It needed to last. A history of this region cannot exclude the explicitly Christian language used by its founders to draw citizens. With a focus on morality, they fostered the kind of virtues they thought would preserve the town as a stable community and productive center of business. The Chambers lived and served according to the Christian ethic on which the town was formed. They were just the kind of people the town founders sought to attract, people who would build Colorado Springs to last for years to come.

The Chambers' story provides a clear window into the first two-and-a-half decades of Colorado Springs history. The themes of their lives align with the themes of their community: health-seeking, agriculture, and the moral culture of the town. Colorado Springs was not a typical frontier town, and the Rock Ledge House and its inhabitants leave a record that explores many unique elements of the region that differ from the average story of settlement in the West. At the same time, however, many challenges and developments within the Chambers' personal history are characteristic of the West. They can teach about universal experiences among pioneers during this period of westward expansion.

As settlers who arrived after the railroad had reached their place of settlement, the Chambers represent a different kind of pioneer than those who travelled across the plains in covered wagons. Yet eventually these post-railroad pioneers and the accompanying developments transformed life in the West. Examining the lives of the Chambers family in their years at Rock Ledge Ranch thus reveals important themes in Colorado Springs history, Colorado history, and the history of the western United States during the last quarter of the nineteenth century. It exposes details about motivations, problems, victories, philosophies, and trends that might not be visible from another perspective. For this reason, the Chambers' story is well worth telling. Through their Rock Ledge House, Elsie W. Chambers and her family were making history by providing the people of the future a unique window into the stories of the past.

Chapter One

"The Most Attractive Place for Homes in the West"
Colorado as the Chambers Knew It

When the Chambers family—Robert, Elsie, Benjamin, and Eleanor—arrived in
Colorado Springs in 1874, they did not clamber out of a wagon onto a dusty,
empty plain. They disembarked from a train into a wealthy resort town with
established newspapers, schools, and churches, for one wave of settlers had already
made its mark on the Pikes Peak region. Just fifteen years prior, only the Native
Americans and occasional white explorers who roamed through it knew this land.
How did this development happen? What made Colorado and Colorado Springs
what they were when the Chambers arrived? The settlement of Colorado by whites
began in Denver and spread west, north, and south, with most important
developments accompanying the railroad. This is a story of big dreams that
sometimes came to fruition and of enticing names that were not always completely
truthful.

Before whites began to settle in Colorado, it was home to dozens of tribes of
Native Americans. Forty-nine Native tribes have ties to Colorado. The Ute people
were the first to call Colorado home, and they had been hunting throughout the
Colorado, Utah, and northern New Mexico area for thousands of years. Because of
the movement of other tribes, by the time the white men explored Colorado, the

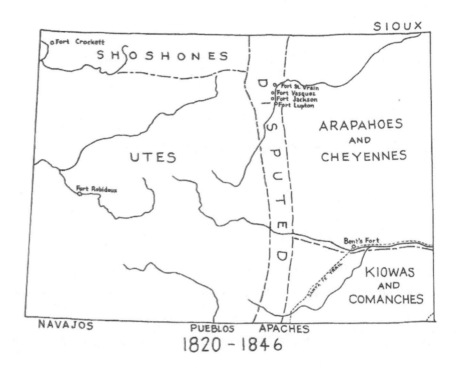

Figure 1 - Native American Tribes in Colorado.
J. Donald Hughes, American Indians in Colorado (Denver: University of Denver, 1977) 75.

lands the Utes mainly inhabited were reduced to central and western Colorado.[2] This can be seen in Figure 1. The Arapaho peoples, pushed west from the Great Lakes as settlers moved there from the East, resided in northeastern Colorado. So did the Cheyenne, who had been driven west from the Minnesota and North Dakota area. The Cheyenne and Arapaho lived as plains tribes, chasing herds of bison in the region of the Platte River.[3] Southeastern Colorado was home to tribes of Kiowas and Comanches. All these tribes considered the Garden of the Gods

---

[2] Carl Abbott, Stephen J. Leonard, and Thomas J. Noel, *Colorado: A History of the Centennial State, Fifth Edition* (Boulder, CO: University Press of Colorado, 2013), 18.

[3] Abbott, Leonard, and Noel, 20.

and the springs at Manitou in the foothills of Pikes Peak to be sacred places of peace.[4] All these lands would eventually be threatened by settlers from the East, but the initial white men who moved into their territory came from the West.

Westward expansion is typically thought of as the gradual movement of explorers and then settlers across the Great Plains west to the Rockies and then to the Pacific Coast. Although this is not wrong, perhaps one of the greatest ironies of westward expansion is that it was at the same time a movement eastward. Prior to the late 1850s, westward expansion was typically either "all the way" to the Pacific Ocean or "just barely" into the West. Nearly all pioneers who set out for the West either travelled past the Rockies to Oregon and California on the West Coast or settled in the states immediately west of the Mississippi River. Some pushed as far as Kansas, especially in the mid-1850s, but the stretch of land between Kansas and California held little attraction for settlers. The Rocky Mountains were enough trouble just to pass through—who would want to endure those frigid winters and dry summers on that rocky soil? Immigrants pushed beyond the mountain territories, considering them useless, in order to reach the fertile soil and gold fields of the West Coast.

Fever first settled the West Coast: Oregon fever and gold fever. Americans in the 1840s rushed all the way across the nation to settle in Oregon, which early pioneers promoted as beautiful, fertile, and restorative for the sick. Thousands of Oregon trail immigrants passed through what many called the Great American Desert and over the Rocky Mountains, trudging all the way to the Oregon Valley to begin farming there. The discovery of gold at Sutter's Mill, California, in 1849 brought a different kind of pioneer: 80,000 miners in the first year alone who intended to strike it rich and then return to their homes in the East.[5] Whether they did find enough shiny metal to fill their pockets to satisfaction or not, east was the

---

[4] Nancy E Loe, *Life in the Altitudes: An Illustrated History of Colorado Springs, First edition* (Woodland Hills, CA: Windsor Publications, 1983), 11.

[5] H.W. Brands, *Dreams of El Dorado: A History of the American West, First edition* (New York: Basic Books, 2019), 231.

only way to go when the gold began to run out. After gold mining in California, both successful and unsuccessful prospectors headed back to the East. Some continued to seek fortune in the territories they travelled through on the way. They discovered gold and silver in Nevada and in Colorado during the late 1850s, then in Idaho in the early 1860s.[6] Precious metals appeared to be the best way to alert the country to the value to be found in the forgotten middle territories of the nation that constitute modern-day Montana, Wyoming, and Colorado.

Meanwhile, farmers from the eastern states who had been pushing steadily west for the entire history of the nation moved even faster and farther after the Homestead Act of 1862. By the beginning of the Civil War, Americans had settled land as far as eastern Kansas and Nebraska. Yet up to this point, moving west had only been an option for those with the money to buy a piece of federal land.[7] The offer of free land through homesteading opened the West up to those who could not previously afford to buy the land on the frontier. Individuals quickly pushed west and staked out their claims. The 1862 Homestead Act was similar to the act that had granted free land to immigrants who travelled to Oregon in the 1840s: a head of household could receive 160 acres of free land if he or she could live on it and improve it for five years. Homesteaders staked out claims farther and farther west into Kansas and Nebraska, which possessed excellent conditions for fruitful farming. The middle section of the country, which had long been passed through but rarely considered good land, began to become home for farmers from the East and miners from the West.[8]

Despite the farming potential, gold was necessary to capture the nation's attention. The land that is now the state of Colorado was a territory one travelled through, not to, until the Pikes Peak Gold Rush. Somewhat deceptive in name, this

---

[6] Brands, *Dreams of El Dorado*, 334.

[7] Brands, 289. One important exception is Texas, which had attracted many settlers because Mexico had offered a homestead policy that made land free.

[8] Mostly. As will be explained shortly, discoveries of gold brought people from both East and West.

discovery occurred not on the Peak, nor even truly in the Pikes Peak region, but instead seventy miles north along the easternmost range of the Rocky Mountains (called the Front Range).[9] One can see the distance from Denver to Pikes Peak in the Figure 2 map on page 18. Explorers and gold miners led by William Green Russell, returning to the East from California, found pockets of the precious metal in the South Platte River, near Cherry Creek, in the summer of 1858. The promise of riches served as an excellent catalyst for news to travel quickly, and miners began to scramble west as word of "The New Eldorado" sped east.[10] Miners and those who set up shop to feed, house, and equip them established Denver by the fall of 1858. Through the winter, those residents engaged in "boosterism:" writing glowing reports of the riches to be found in "Pikes Peak Country." As soon as the weather allowed in 1859, the roads near the South Platte were packed with Pikes Peak immigrants. Some towns back East along the Missouri River reported seventy-five to a hundred wagons passing through them every day in April and May, all of them headed for the Peak.[11] The nation had found a reason to settle Colorado—or had they?

---

[9] One reason for this misnomer may be the fact that Pikes Peak has a curious ability to appear close from far away, and it is visible from very far north and east of the peak. Explorer Zebulon Pike discovered this optical illusion that makes the peak seem close even when one is still very far away, and it resulted in his never actually making it up the peak because he severely underestimated how far away it was. If "Pikes Peak Country" just meant the areas within which one can see the peak, then perhaps the Pikes Peak Gold Rush was not far from being in Pikes Peak Country—though it still is quite a journey from the peak itself.

[10] Abbott, Leonard, and. Noel, *Colorado: A History of the Centennial State,* 45.

[11] Ibid., 49.

18

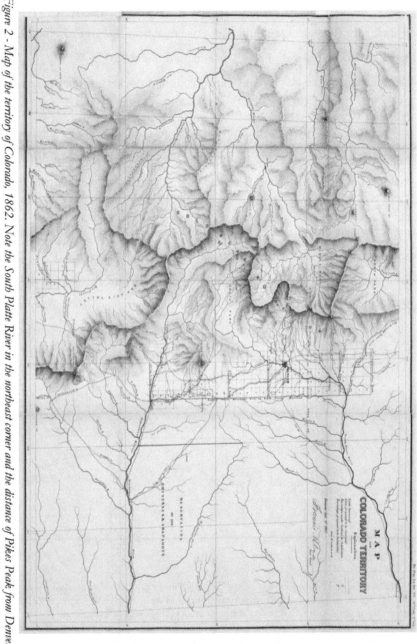

Figure 2 - Map of the territory of Colorado, 1862. Note the South Platte River in the northeast corner and the distance of Pikes Peak from Denver. Map drawn by Francis M. Case. The Denver Public Library, Western History Collection, CG4310 1862 .C3.

Cries of "Pikes Peak or Bust" in April became "Cherry Creek and Busted" by June. There was not nearly as much gold in the South Platte as the optimistic boosters had promised. Many who had eagerly scurried west turned heel and plodded back home, counseling other immigrants to turn back as they went. Some estimate the numbers of "go-backers" as high as 40,000 migrants. This was probably more than eighty percent of those who rushed to Denver because of the gold mania. Denver's population remained around 3,000 people, scarcely larger than it had been at the start of the year.[12] Meanwhile, men determined to succeed (or unwilling to go back) kept mining and began to uncover larger deposits of ore deeper in the mountains. Though some were hesitant to believe more cries of gold, the rush began again that summer and by August some 10,000 gold seekers were mining in Colorado.[13] Though no longer at the heart of the gold discoveries, Denver prospered as a stocking up and refueling town.

The Cheyenne and Arapaho tribes who lived out on the eastern Colorado plains were the first to clash with the settlers coming west. In the first few years, relatively little conflict arose. The Cheyenne and Arapaho did not covet the gold that the miners were furiously panning for, and the gold seekers did not threaten the natives. By the mid 1860s, however, white men began to seize more and more land, leaving the natives fewer and fewer hunting grounds.[14] Eventually whites displaced the peoples who had lived out on the plains and in the foothills. The 1861 Treaty of Fort Wise replaced the 1851 Treaty of Fort Laramie, taking away Arapaho and Cheyenne rights to northeastern Colorado. The tribes initially accepted this, but violence escalated to a climax in the 1864 Sand Creek Massacre, when Colonel John Chivington opened fire on a Cheyenne and Arapaho encampment, killing 170 natives. Occasional violence continued until the 1867 Treaty of Medicine Lodge,

---

[12]Abbott, Leonard, and. Noel, *Colorado: A History of the Centennial State*. Compare this to San Francisco, which had grown from 1,000 citizens to 25,000 from 1848-1849, when its gold rush happened.

[13] Ibid., 52.

[14] Ibid., 82-83.

20

which stipulated that the Cheyenne and Arapaho remove to Oklahoma.[15] Meanwhile, the Ute, who roamed in the more mountainous regions of Colorado, would remain protected from losing their land for another fifteen years.

This was not really Colorado yet, however. What is now Colorado was at this point split between the Kansas, Nebraska, Utah, and New Mexico territories. Instead of one government, the land was managed by over one hundred mining districts, which were the only means of regulating mining claims and punishing criminals.[16] Eager to establish a more consistent form of government, settlers south of Denver in the Pikes Peak region voted to request territorial status and began the process of organizing a territorial government. The national government at first refused, but in early 1861, with the chaos of Southern secession looming, President James Buchanan signed into existence the Colorado Territory, named after the Colorado River. Territorial status meant Colorado citizens could not elect their own governor and high officials nor send voting representatives to Congress, but they could elect their own legislature and they need not pay taxes.[17] Colorado was on its way to statehood. It was not until 1876, however, that Colorado became the thirty-eighth state in the union and gained the name "the Centennial State" for attaining statehood on the country's one-hundredth birthday.

Because Colorado was still a frontier community struggling to retain settlers, the work of boosters and promoters was an absolute necessity to keep the territory alive. The Civil War years saw a decline in the population, despite the 1862 Homestead Act. Mining towns swiftly turned to ghost towns when lodes were exhausted, and even Denver decreased in population. To stay afloat, Colorado citizens needed to draw attention to their territory and bring more waves of pioneers who would hopefully become permanent residents. Colorado newspapers set to work once more promoting Colorado, sending men as far as Paris to show

---

[15] Abbott, Leonard, and. Noel, *Colorado: A History of the Centennial State*, 85-86.

[16] Thomas J Noel, Paul F Mahoney, and Richard E Stevens, *Historical Atlas of Colorado* (Norman: University of Oklahoma Press, 1993), 34.

[17] Abbot, Leonard, and Noel, *Colorado: A History of the Centennial State*, 58.

off the resources of the region.[18] Many, such as territorial governor William Gilpin, painted Colorado as the future focal point of the continent, trying to entice settlers with descriptions of the clean mountain air and the benefits of irrigation-driven farming in Colorado's dry climate.

If the territory was to grow and eventually achieve statehood, however, it needed to be able to transport people there more quickly than wagons or stagecoaches could. Denver's population still lagged below 5,000 people, not at all the growth the territory's promoters had wanted to see in its first ten years. At first, the national plans for the transcontinental railroad seemed like they would solve the trials of travel to the territory. Coloradans assumed that Denver would be a main stop on this great national line, connecting it with New York, Chicago, and San Francisco as one of the big cities of the nation. The railroad builders, on the other hand, had no such plans. They were granted federal funding per mile of track laid—and a mile of flat land makes for easier laying than a mile of Rocky Mountains. Another related factor was the need for speed: the Union Pacific and Central Pacific were competing against each other to lay more track and earn more government money.[19] It would cost too much time and materials to lay tracks through the Colorado Rockies. The Union Pacific was better off building its rails through the less mountainous Wyoming (see map, Figure 3, on page 22).[20] The transcontinental railroad would not unite Denver with both coasts after all.

Colorado would be left out of the national railroad unless its people took matters into their own hands. This caused great dismay among the Denverites who had pictured themselves and their fair city as the center of the nation and its glorious transcontinental railroad. To join with the railroad that would soon unite the nation from coast to coast, Colorado businessmen would need to build a railroad themselves. The idea of a north-south spur railroad had not been entirely

---

[18] Abbott, Leonard, and. Noel, *Colorado: A History of the Centennial State.*, 68.

[19] Brands, *Dreams of El Dorado,* 291.

[20] Abbot, Leonard, and Noel, *Colorado: A History of the Centennial State,* 72.

22

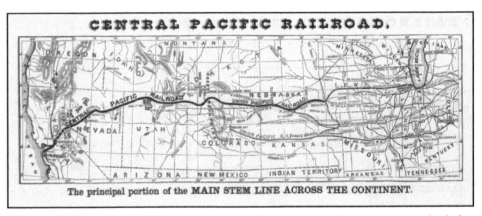

The principal portion of the **MAIN STEM LINE ACROSS THE CONTINENT.**

Figure 3 - The Transcontinental Railroad passed north of Colorado through Wyoming, so a spur line had to be built from Denver to Cheyenne. (Map from American-rails.com.)

neglected, but suddenly it became a necessity of the present, not just a pretty idea for the future.[21] The Colorado Central Railroad of Golden and the Denver Pacific Railroad began to compete in 1868 to lay one hundred miles of track that would connect Denver with the Union Pacific in Cheyenne. This endeavor created more than just train tracks—it founded towns along the tracks as they went north from Colorado into Wyoming.[22] The Denver Pacific eventually won out, and by mid-1870 Denver was reachable via train from Cheyenne. Denver would not be cut out of the network after all. It is on this spur line that the Chambers family would ride from Cheyenne to Denver in April 1874—but the line that would one day take them to their destination further south had yet to be constructed.

The same year that Denver connected with the transcontinental railroad, tracks reached Denver from the East. Though perhaps less exciting to Denver citizens, this development proved vastly important for the establishment of Colorado Springs. The Kansas Pacific railroad from Kansas City plowed into Denver at record speed in August 1870, under the direction of General William Jackson Palmer. Palmer, a veteran of the Civil War, was a driven and enthusiastic young railroad man who had previously been tasked with surveying the Colorado territory

---

[21] O. Meredith Wilson, *The Denver and Rio Grande Project, 1870-1901: A History of the First Thirty Years of the Denver and Rio Grande Railroad* (Salt Lake City: Westwater Press, 1981), 3.

[22] *Historical Atlas of Colorado*, 28.

for a way to the Pacific from Kansas. Taking the railroad through Denver, however, had not been his goal. After spending 1867 and 1868 exploring southern Colorado on behalf of the Kansas Pacific Railroad, Palmer had written reports attempting to persuade the Kansas Pacific to take a more southern route. He recommended that they build southwest to Pueblo, Colorado, some one hundred fifteen miles south of Denver and proceed from there west to California along the thirty-fifth parallel.[23] Palmer pressed enthusiastically for this route, but the company and Congress (on which the company was depending for the funds to build this railroad) were not convinced. Short on money, the Kansas Pacific would instead build to Denver and find their connection to California through the Union Pacific railroad.[24]

Despite his disappointment at his plan's rejection, Palmer took on the job of directing the construction of the railroad to Denver. Because of difficulties getting materials and motivating laborers in Kansas, progress in laying tracks had slowed to a halt about 230 miles away from Denver.[25] Palmer took the project in hand and shocked everyone with the speed and efficiency his crews achieved: the last one hundred fifty miles of track to Denver were laid in one hundred fifty days, and the last ten miles in just ten hours.[26] By mid-August 1870, a train from Kansas City chugged into Denver—now a two-railroad town. Even though one could not merely hop on the transcontinental railroad and reach Denver without ever switching trains, it was possible to ride the rails to Denver.

Palmer had not dropped his dreams of a railroad to the south, however, and he discovered in Denver that there were others who shared his interests in both a railroad and a town to the south. Palmer began to write to his future bride, Mary

---

[23] Wilson, 5.

[24] Ibid.

[25] Ibid.

[26] Ibid., 6.

Lincoln "Queen" Mellen, about his dreams of "Our Road."[27] His vision of uniting Denver with Santa Fe, New Mexico, by rail was more than grasping an economic opportunity or filling a transportation need. He desired a railroad that would allow him and his friends to live in a new community at the base of the beautiful Front Range. This would one day be Colorado Springs, a community carefully designed to avoid the instability so often present in frontier railroad towns.[28] Almost as soon as he had accomplished his duty with the Kansas Pacific Railroad in Denver, Palmer began organizing his own railroad, first reserving the land he wanted to build through and then forming the Denver and Rio Grande Railroad. The people of Denver, who had seen Palmer's passionate and energetic efficiency in getting the railroad to Denver, were supportive of his next goal to extend the railroad south.

Raising funds would be no small task, however, for the money market for railroading at this time was tight. Palmer needed to acquire significant funding from private investors—a task he succeeded at impressively. Money raised from friends of Palmer's contributed a large portion of the needed finances, as did funding from friends of Dr. William Bell, an Englishman who managed to successfully sell both the railroad stocks and Colorado itself to many interested individuals across the pond.[29] One way Palmer raised money for his railroad was by requiring those who wished to purchase the land he had acquired for the new settlement to become subscribers to the railroad.[30] Yet to interest English investors who were wary of railroad investments, Palmer's Denver and Rio Grande Railroad needed to be able to construct their tracks cheaply.[31] They accomplished this by narrowing the width of the track they laid.

---

[27] Wilson, 6.

[28] Abbot, Leonard, and Noel, *Colorado: A History of the Centennial State*, 77.

[29] Wilson, 11.

[30] Ibid., 15.

[31] Ibid., 13.

The Denver and Rio Grande Railroad was the first true narrow-gauge railroad in the country. There was not one standard width for railroad tracks in 1870, though the question of whether there should be had come up for debate. Congress and the president had required that the transcontinental railroad be built with the 4-foot 8.5-inch gauge because a significant majority of tracks in the United States at the time were 4 feet, 8.5 inches wide. Yet no laws stipulated that all tracks be the same standard width. It is unknown at what point Palmer and the Denver and Rio Grande decided to build the railroad on a narrower gauge, but the decision was certainly a wise one when it came to gaining English investors. Building a railroad less than five feet wide cut the cost down to two-thirds of the price for normal gauge railroads.[32] It also was a wise decision considering the terrain they needed to overcome. Laying tracks along the Front Range might pose some difficulties, but those were nothing compared to what the Denver and Rio Grande would encounter once it entered the mountains. A narrower gauge would be able to handle tighter curves and steeper grades—challenges that would be plentiful in the Rockies.

Palmer once again proved that he could accomplish a feat quickly, for his team had the railroad from Denver to Colorado Springs ready in just a year's time. Grading for the railroad began on March 1, 1871. Despite the high costs of both iron and labor in Colorado, by the end of July the land had been graded and construction crews were laying tracks, working at a rate of about two miles per ten-hour workday.[33] By October 1871, the tracks reached from Denver to the base of Pikes Peak, and by January of 1872, regular business exchange between Denver and the growing settlement that would become Colorado Springs began. (See map of the Denver and Rio Grande Raikway, Figure 4 on page 26.)

---

[32] *Historical Atlas of Colorado*, 28.

[33] Wilson, 18.

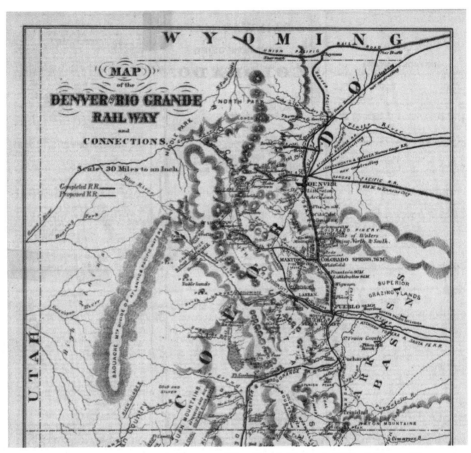

Figure 4 - Map of the plans for the Denver and Rio Grande Railroad, 1873. (Library of Congress)

This region in the shadow of Pikes Peak had held several failed settlements previously. In 1858, some of the miners who had failed to find gold at Cherry Creek had travelled seventy miles south, hoping that the actual Pikes Peak would not bust them the same way the Pikes Peak Gold Rush had. Their hopes were unrealized, for although they planned the town of El Paso nestled in the foothills before the Front Range, it never actually came into existence. Later that same year, another group of settlers arrived and attempted to start a town they called Eldorado in the same place, but they too never got as far as constructing any buildings. The third time was the charm—another group of settlers founded a new town in 1859, this time calling it Colorado City.[34]

Though it had taken a few tries to start up a settlement there, the location of Colorado City was judicious for several reasons. First, it was at the base of Ute Pass, the "gateway around the peak" which had been blazed by Indians and that settlers now used to traverse past the Front Range and back into the Rocky Mountains.[35] With regard to geography and weather, Colorado City was protected from the dangerous Front Range winds by the large natural mesa to the north.[36] Thus, it was an ideal place for those mining up in the colder mountain regions to spend the winter. Like Denver, though obviously on a much smaller scale, Colorado City became a place to stock up on necessities before entering the mountains. By 1862 the town boasted three hundred citizens, including some farmers as well as miners and merchants.[37] Yet the decade from 1862-1871 was a struggle for this small town—no surprise during the Civil War years. Though some homesteaders settled in the area, the population did not grow much beyond three hundred people. Colorado City briefly served as the territorial capital, but those serving in the legislature found the rustic accommodations to be less than satisfactory. They swiftly moved their meetings to Denver.[38] Palmer's railroad would revive the area, but he had a vision far larger than just growing Colorado City. He had plans for a new town.

More than just a new town, Palmer envisioned the Pikes Peak region as the perfect location for a beautiful health resort for citizens and visitors of the highest quality. Palmer loved the Colorado Springs area. While previous explorers had declared the area "almost wholly unfit for cultivation," Palmer saw the land as ideal

---

[34] Loe, 17. At this time, the whole area that is now called Colorado was still part of Kansas territory. Colorado City was named before the territory it was in was called Colorado.

[35] Ibid., 17.

[36] *Historical Atlas of Colorado,* 5.

[37] Loe, 17.

[38] Ibid., 17-18.

for agriculture and pasturage.[39] He also praised the dry air and mild winters of the area as perfect for those needing relief from humid and dirty Eastern cities. Palmer's survey of the region in the late 1860s had ignited in him a dream not just for a new business and new settled territory through the railroad, but for a new community. His years spent working on the railroad had opened his eyes to the many vices of frontier towns that caused their downfall. He had a vision of a better society of fair exchange, good relations between employers and employees, and law-abiding citizens. By owning the land along the railroad, his company could ensure that the city that sprung up at the base of Pikes Peak was the kind of steady, prosperous place he desired.[40] Buying the land on the prairie in front of the Peak from the government for only eighty cents an acre, Palmer and his team originally named his new community the Fountain Colony. Yet he quickly seized on a more appealing name: Colorado Springs.

Once again, names can be deceptive. Colorado Springs proper held no springs. It was, however, about five miles away from an area with several springs that Native Americans called Manitou, closer to the base of Pikes Peak (west of Colorado City). The springs of Manitou would help make Colorado Springs an appealing destination for those travelling for the sake of their health. Following the example of General Cameron's Greeley colony, a town north of Denver which had pioneered the practice of carefully organized colony towns, Palmer organized the Colorado Springs Company. Into it he brought a group of individuals who planned, organized, and invested money in the town-to-be, to begin to improve the land he had already acquired for his city. The colony model meant that Colorado Springs was founded with the intent of creating a sustainable business. Restrictions like that of no alcohol were intended to keep the town stable and productive. The company was organized to work like a well-oiled machine. Palmer provided the vision and raised the money, delegating other men to work out the details. A man from his Civil War cavalry regiment, Major Henry McAllister, sold land in

---

[39] Loe, 16, and Abbot, Leonard, and Noel, *Colorado: A History of the Centennial State*, 76.

[40] Abbot, Leonard, and Noel, *Colorado: A History of the Centennial State*, 79.

Philadelphia and raised money for the endeavor before moving his family west to become the executive director of the colony. Money from investors and from the sale of land to members provided the necessary funds to lay out streets, dig irrigation ditches, and bring in trees.[41]

Members of the company not only needed the funds to purchase and improve land, but they were required to be "of good moral character and sober habits."[42] Palmer would take no chances on letting his new town become like the frontier towns that he had seen as a railroad man, the towns that had concerned him with their raucous immorality and instability. Colorado Springs would be beautiful, prosperous, and ethical; in the words of Palmer, it was to be "the most attractive place for homes in the West."[43] This was no mining town, nor would it be a factory town. When Palmer extended the Denver and Rio Grande railway down to the already existing city of Pueblo, he founded a new town there (named, with outstanding originality, South Pueblo) that swiftly became the productive factory city for the region. Colorado Springs, on the other hand, would not hold factories; it was a town for the well-to-do who were morally upright. The Colorado Springs Company decided that the best way to attract the kind of citizens they wanted was to start with education and religion as the most important features.[44] Setting aside land for churches and prohibiting the production or sale of alcohol within city limits were just two of the ways they sought to bring in stable and upstanding citizens and set Colorado Springs apart from the wild and raucous frontier towns. The Colorado Springs Company broke ground in July of 1871, a few months before Colorado Springs could be reached by railroad.

---

[41] Loe, 20, and Abbot, Leonard, and Noel, *Colorado: A History of the Centennial State*, 79. The area that is now Colorado Springs was, as mentioned earlier, prairie when Palmer arrived. The cottonwood trees that now grow in the city were brought in by the Colorado Springs Company and initially tended by professional gardeners.

[42] Abbot, Leonard, and Noel, *Colorado: A History of the Centennial State*, 79.

[43] Ibid.

[44] Gregory Atkins, "'Business Sense If Not Souls': Boosters and Religion in Colorado Springs, 1871-1909" (*The Journal of the Gilded Age and Progressive Era* 17, no. 1, 2018), 79.

The "boosterism" advertising Colorado Springs as a "model resort community" succeeded in bringing citizens west. By early 1872, eight hundred residents resided in the town, only six months after the Colorado Springs Company had broken ground. By the end of that same year, the population had nearly doubled to 1,500.[45] Many of the first citizens of Colorado Springs were friends whom Henry McAllister recruited in Pennsylvania or whom Dr William Bell brought from England. In fact, so many residents came from Great Britain that Colorado Springs displayed some decidedly British habits in its first ten years. Afternoon tea at four was an absolute given, and the local papers printed far more international news than most papers out West did at the time. The British influence was so pervasive in the first several years that the city gained the nickname "Little London."[46] Colorado Springs certainly possessed upper-class taste as well. Early colonists came so quickly that a few hundred portable houses had to be shipped in by train for them to live in until more permanent structures could be constructed.[47] One sharp-witted resident published an editorial in the local paper, commenting: "Our streets are being adorned with some ready-made structures from Chicago. Such a style of architecture may do for Chicago, but if she send us many more specimens of it, we shall petition her to send us also a cow and some kerosene."[48] Palmer's vision of an upper-class resort community with upper-class tastes was coming into being, thanks to the steady work of Cameron, McAllister, and other Colorado Springs Company organizers.

What of the Native Americans who once roamed the land? The Utes held out in the mountains for many years and maintained mostly good relations with the people of Colorado City and Colorado Springs for the first few decades, despite the anti-Native sentiments and actions of many whites. The Utes even trekked

---

[45] Abbot, Leonard, and Noel, *Colorado: A History of the Centennial State,* 79.

[46] Loe, 22.

[47] Wilson, 20.

[48] Loe, 20. Considering that the Great Chicago Fire which this clever comment references had happened only about a year ago in 1871, this statement seems a little insensitive.

down the pass into Colorado City to trade for many years. Throughout the 1870s it would not have been uncommon for citizens of Colorado City to see Ute people in and around town. As settlers continued to push west into the mountains, however, they began to resent the agreements that the U.S. government had made with the Utes. Whites continued to carve away at protected Ute lands and in 1876 began to petition the government to remove the Utes to Oklahoma. Nathan Meeker, a Colorado pioneer unsuccessfully trying to teach the Utes agriculture, called in the army when a native assailed him. Fearing removal by the soldiers, the Utes attacked, killing ten soldiers, Meeker, and some civilians in what became known as the Meeker Massacre of 1879. This only gave those who advocated for Ute removal more fodder, and in 1880 and 1881, the Utes were forced to move to Utah.[49] Thus by 1880, most interactions between the citizens of Colorado Springs and the Native American peoples that had once dwelt in that area were over.

The location and scenery made Colorado Springs a popular tourist destination—for the right price. The transcontinental railroad made reaching Colorado possible for those with enough money for a train ticket, and Colorado quickly became an extremely popular vacation spot. Colorado Springs was less attainable than Denver, not so much because it was farther away but because it was so expensive. Designed to be a resort town for those of the upper classes, it could hold many guests in its luxurious hotels as long as those guests had heavy pocketbooks.[50] Boosters acknowledged the costliness but noted that it was well worth it, because in Colorado Springs one could live an "Eastern life in a Western environment."[51] They were not incorrect: in Colorado Springs Eastern social life with all its Victorian propriety occurred in an undeniably Western landscape with many opportunities for exploration. Visible from everywhere in the city, Pikes Peak had long held fascination for explorers. Now, it was reachable for those with a

[49] Abbot, Leonard, and Noel, *Colorado: A History of the Centennial State*, 90.

[50] Ibid., 227.

[51] Ibid., 227.

sense of adventure but perhaps not the same appreciation for ruggedness. Tourists
could reach the top by mule, wagon, their own two feet, or eventually by the Cog
Railway. If that was too strenuous, they could hike through the nearby canyons to
take picnics and visit waterfalls.

Even closer to the city, just slightly north of Manitou, lay another wonder:
the Garden of the Gods. The massive red rocks towering up out of the ground had
long been considered a sacred place to the Ute people who claimed this area as
their home.[52] Early explorers expressed similar awe at the large sandstone
formations. According to most sources, the Garden acquired its name when one of
the founders of Colorado City commented to his companion that it would be an
excellent place for a beer garden. Appalled, his friend rejected the notion
immediately, insisting instead that "it is a fit place for the Gods to assemble. We
will call it the Garden of the Gods."[53] The Garden became an immensely popular
tourist attraction, and those with a mind for business quickly found ways to make
money from eager Eastern sightseers. Guided tours and photographs in front of
Balanced Rock (as in Figure 5 on page 33) were only a few options for those
desiring adventures in nature a little closer to their resorts. Though the property
was purchased by Charles Elliott Perkins in 1879, the Garden remained open to
the public and Perkins never built on it, bequeathing it to the city upon his death
so that it would remain free to the public.[54] General Palmer himself constructed his
home, Glen Eyrie, inside a canyon just north of Garden of the Gods, which was
desirable land not just for the scenery but also for the water that flowed down the
canyon he named Queen's Canyon, for his wife.

---

[52] Loe, 11.

[53] Irving Howbert, *Memories of a Lifetime in the Pike's Peak Region* (Glorieta, N.M: Rio Grande Press, 1970), 83.

[54] Howbert, *Memories of a Lifetime in the Pike's Peak Region*, 293.

Those with enough money to do so came to Colorado Springs for more than just the scenery—many came chasing a cure. Tourists sought the springs of Manitou for the "water cure" that they hoped the natural springs would provide. The water cure, a national obsession in the late nineteenth century for those suffering from various ailments, attracted many to the Colorado Springs area. The climate also proved to be a powerful draw to Colorado Springs, one that boosters capitalized on just as much as the gorgeous landscapes. The dryness of the air, combined with the elevation above

Figure 5 - Woman on mule in front of Balanced Rock, c. 1900. There are hundreds of photos like this one with tourists in front of the rock formation. (Bluefiremark Graphic Design Studio.)

sea level and the large number of sunny days, was thought to help if not absolutely cure lung problems. The winters, though still cold, were not as damp as they were in the East, providing relief to consumptives. Consumption, also known as tuberculosis, was a rampant problem during the latter half of the nineteenth century for which doctors recommended heading west to escape the humidity, grime, and overcrowding of Eastern cities. Colorado in general, but especially Colorado Springs, drew thousands of sufferers with the promise of the climate cure. One Colorado Springs doctor who specialized in tuberculosis, Dr. Samuel Edwin Solly, wrote that "it is often estimated that a third of the population came for their health or that of their families, and probably the estimate is not excessive."[55] Verifying the precision of such an estimate is impossible, but there is

---

[55] Loe, 27.

no doubt that the health seekers who flocked to Colorado and especially to Colorado Springs constituted a sizeable percentage of the population.[56] The Colorado Springs area swiftly became a health resort for the wealthy.

Between gold-seekers, health-seekers, friends of the founders, and others who responded to the boosterism that promoted Colorado Springs, the city grew remarkably fast. By 1874, just three years after its founding, "Little London" boasted 3,000 citizens.[57] By 1878, the town could host as many as 25,000 guests in its hotels and boardinghouses.[58] The next available population data comes from the 1885 Colorado census, which records 8,356 people living in El Paso County, with 4,563 of them abiding in Colorado Springs proper.[59] Far from the ready-made structures that had first adorned the streets, the wealthy residential section of the North End of Colorado Springs had turned the barren and dusty prairie into a lovely and life-filled neighborhood. Visitors from the East were shocked at the beauty of the cottonwood trees and gardens, all watered by an irrigation system that ran along the sidewalks.[60] One guest called it a "charming big village" filled with buildings possessing "an air of comfort."[61] The Colorado Springs Company had planned it out well, and their wide streets were filling up not just with homes, but with churches, schools, and even a college. Five public schools and several private ones served over seven hundred students by the winter of 1885, and Colorado College, which was founded in 1874, had about fifty students.[62] Socially,

---

[56] The fact that by 1885, Missouri, New York, Illinois, Ohio, Pennsylvania, and Iowa contributed the most citizens to Colorado Springs perhaps helps bolster this estimation, for those were humid states where the cold and damp would be considered dangerous for consumptives. It is also true, however, that these states experienced "the greatest attacks of gold fever in 1859," so one cannot be sure how many of these came for gold versus their health. Loe, *Life in the Altitudes,* 39.

[57] Abbot, Leonard, and Noel, *Colorado: A History of the Centennial State,* 79.

[58] Ibid., 227.

[59] Loe, 39.

[60] Ibid., 46.

[61] Ibid., 49.

[62] Ibid., 54.

the town was providing all the improvements the colony's founders had wanted to make this an anti-frontier town.

Improvements in resources, comforts, and technology came quickly as well. Though for a time most foods were more expensive in Colorado Springs than they were back East, by 1885 some goods, such as flour and poultry, could be acquired for less money than in Eastern cities, because trains were arriving more frequently.[63] Shockingly modern developments came quickly to this new town. Telephones began to become available in 1880. In 1885, citizens could have gas lighting installed in their homes.[64] Locals could acquire news through any of six weekly papers, though most did so chiefly through the *Gazette*, which had been around since 1872.[65] Colorado Springs was clearly not a typical frontier town; it was a town that could rival many Eastern cities less than fifteen years after its founding with its fast-growing population and technology.

The next fifteen years saw continued population growth, but the depression that the nation experienced after the panic of 1893 hit Colorado hard. The combination of the decline of silver (because of the repeal of the Sherman Silver Purchase Act) and of farm prices spelled disaster for citizens all over the state.[66] For everyone from bankers to farmers to railroad men, the 1890s were tough years. From 1889-1890 and again in 1893, Colorado experienced extremely dry seasons which surprised the farmers who had become accustomed to the unusually high rainfall of the 1870s and 1880s.[67] Economic depression meant less leisure travel, and thus the railroads had to find ways to motivate people to become passengers.

---

[63] Loe, 54.

[64] Ibid., 53.

[65] Ibid.

[66] Brands, *Dreams of El Dorado,* 442. The Sherman Silver Purchase Act resulted in the government buying lots of silver, which of course made silver even more valuable and plumped the pockets of those involved in the silver mining industry across the nation. Its repeal meant that silver fell dramatically in price, reducing many miners and others to poverty. Abbot, Leonard, and Noel, *Colorado: A History of the Centennial State*, 114.

[67] Abbot, Leonard, and Noel, *Colorado: A History of the Centennial State*, 174-175.

They printed postcards and pamphlets as promptly as possible and offered discounted rates for travel. Thus in the midst of a nationwide depression, travel by rail became more accessible to the middle class of society.[68] This led to not only more middle-class visitors but also more middle class residents in Colorado Springs. The city's population increased five-fold from 1880 to 1900, growing from 4,226 to 21,085.[69] Colorado Springs was no longer just a wealthy resort town. Although it was certainly not the frontier town the company had wanted to avoid, it was now a far less homogenous society.

Much population growth in these years was also due to the Cripple Creek Gold Rush of 1891. Though Pikes Peak had long been considered only a place of hoax gold rushes, one stubbornly determined miner had kept looking until he had found a true lode. This increased the population of Colorado Springs in two opposing directions. Those who had struck it rich descended from the mountains to build opulent homes in the North End. Meanwhile, the Colorado Springs Aid Society noted a marked increase in families so poor they needed help to survive.[70] Financial struggle and yet growth seems to describe the final decade of the nineteenth century in Colorado and Colorado Springs.

In less than fifty years, Colorado had changed from an almost unknown territory in the middle of the United States to a state known and loved for its resources, scenery, and climate. The first wave of pioneers had explored, mapped and begun settling so that the population centers of Denver and Colorado Springs were far from being dusty and uncivilized frontier towns. Colorado Springs had begun as a scrupulously planned colony town and grown from a resort for the wealthy to a home for numerous and diverse settlers. It had much to offer in the way of health, wealth, and good society, if one had the means to establish oneself there.

---

[68] Abbot, Leonard, and Noel, *Colorado: A History of the Centennial State*, 231.

[69] *Historical Atlas of Colorado*, 48.

[70] Loe, 81.

Chapter Two

"A Beautiful Home for an Invalid"
The Chambers Family and Health Seekers in Colorado Springs

Before the railroad arrived at the base of Pikes Peak, a trip to Colorado Springs was not for the faint of heart. Once the city was reachable by train, however, the weak of lung made the trip frequently and in huge numbers. Ailing individuals from across the nation travelled to sunny Colorado Springs, desperately hoping that the newspapers were correct about the miraculous mountain air. Among these hordes of health seekers came Robert and Elsie W. Chambers and their two young children. Swiftly joining the ranks of recovered invalids in Colorado Springs, they set out to provide for other health seekers by opening their home as a boarding house. The theme of health in early Colorado Springs history is woven through the Chambers family's story, from their motivations for leaving Pennsylvania to their years of boarding invalids.

Elsie Woolsey Chambers' health was declining rapidly in the spring of 1874. Ever since the birth of her first daughter Eleanor in 1873, Elsie's constitution had been delicate. Now her family, especially her husband Robert, were growing concerned as this young wife and mother seemed "about to break down."[71] With another baby now on the way, something needed to be done. After losing his first wife in childbirth, Robert Chambers was not going to risk losing

---

[71] Mary Chambers DeLong, "The Chambers Family History," 1.

Elsie if he could do anything to stop it. From the vantage of Limestone Township, Pennsylvania, sunny Colorado seemed to hold the cure.

What exactly ailed Elsie Woolsey Chambers remains uncertain. Her youngest daughter, Mary Chambers DeLong, later wrote that Elsie was "from a T.B. family" and the youngest of eleven children, so the family made assumptions similar to those of tuberculosis patients.[72] The idea that tuberculosis ran in families was an incorrect but widely believed notion in the late 1800s. Although the French surgeon Jean-Antoine Villemin displayed through his experiments in the 1860s that tuberculosis was infectious and not hereditary, this idea was not accepted by most physicians for many years.[73] People still knew little and disputed much about tuberculosis through the 1870s until Berlin scientist Robert Koch discovered the cause of tuberculosis in the early 1880s. Building off the work of Villemin, Koch established that the tubercle bacillus, *Mycobacterium tuberculosis,* infected both humans and animals and caused tuberculosis in different parts of the body.[74] The tubercle bacillus most commonly infects the human lungs, causing symptoms including loss of appetite, fatigue, fever, and cough. Because of the way TB patients lost weight and became weaker as they succumbed to the disease, it was often called consumption.

Many incorrect theories about consumption, such as the one that the disease was inherited by children from their parents, remained part of public belief for years to come. As late as the 1890s, American doctors such as Owen Wister scoffed at the idea that tuberculosis could not be passed down genetically.[75] Those who accepted Koch's findings still pursued curious means of preventing the spread. Today it is known that tuberculosis spreads by means of the dry bacilli coughed into the air, but before the turn of the century, theories about preventing

---

[72] Mary Chambers DeLong, "The Chambers Family History," 1.

[73] Thomas M. Daniel, *Captain of Death: The Story of Tuberculosis* (Rochester, NY, USA: University of Rochester Press, 1997), 71.

[74] Daniel, 80.

[75] Ibid., 90.

the spread of the disease were strange. Some American doctors urged families caring for consumptives to clean the ill person's walls, floors, and ceilings every two weeks, wash their clothes separately, and burn their spit with corrosive sublimate.[76] In short, neither the general public nor the doctors understood tuberculosis very well in the 1800s. Most considered change in climate the best way to combat the disease.

Other than some recorded concern about ancestral consumptives, however, there is nothing that suggests that Elsie W. Chambers suffered from tuberculosis. She was never diagnosed, and even if she had been, many people of this time were misdiagnosed. It was merely established that her health was poor after Eleanor's birth and during her next pregnancy. She herself wrote only that "Mr. R.M. Chambers…[came] to Colorado for his wife's health" and never described her symptoms.[77] It is most likely that Elsie W. Chambers never had tuberculosis.

Nevertheless, family records indicate that the Chambers' move to Colorado was at least connected to tuberculosis. Mary Chambers DeLong later wrote that Robert and Elsie decided on Colorado for their future home because it was "the place for T.B.ers" and because of firsthand accounts from friends.[78] A friend of Elsie's from Normal School, Sarah Carver Wolff, had recently moved to Denver with her husband. She wrote Elsie glowing reports of Colorado and urged the Chambers to join them out West.[79] The rest of the world seemed to agree with the Wolffs. Newspapers across the country sang the praises of Colorado for the relief of many diverse ailments. One example is the *Out West,* the Colorado Springs newspaper later renamed the *Colorado Springs Gazette*. The *Out West* published multiple editorials and essays about the benefits of the Colorado climate. Boosterish writers all but promised that "a few weeks [in Colorado] suffice to set

---

[76] Daniel, 89.

[77] Elsie Woolsey Chambers, "What Happened While the Cabin Lived," 5.

[78] Mary Chambers DeLong, "The Chambers Family History," 1.

[79] Ibid., 1.

on foot the process of improvement, the wasting consumption is checked, bodily vigor, good spirits, appetite, and flesh, all begin to return, and the patient soon finds himself on the way to recovery."[80] Robert and Elsie Chambers perhaps read many similar accounts of the improved health that Colorado brought to the ailing. But why? What was it about Colorado that was supposed to help?

Colorado Springs newspapers of the time sang the praises of the beneficial effects of high altitude, dry air, and sunshine upon those who visited or settled there. Because Colorado Springs sits approximately six thousand feet above sea level, the air itself is thinner and lighter. Breathing is harder work at this high altitude because one does not draw in as much oxygen with each breath. This is a good thing, wrote the editor of the *Out West,* because it requires more rapid breathing, which strengthens the chest and the lungs.[81] Higher altitude requires one to become stronger to survive—this is why many articles of the time urged people with only mild to moderate illnesses to come to Colorado. For the very sick, the altitude would harm rather than help them. The climate was no magic cure-all, and the very weak and those far advanced in lung diseases might die before they could be cured.[82] Though they certainly exaggerated, doctors and boosters were correct that the high altitude could help strengthen the healthy and the sick alike.

The dryness of the climate was also an important factor, especially compared to the humid and polluted air of Eastern cities. Colorado is a high desert with low amounts of precipitation and very low humidity. Doctors argued that the dry air could help cure lung diseases because drier air did not conduct heat and electricity as much as more humid air did.[83] Without fogs, dews, and general damp, the air was purer and easier to breathe. For many, this relieved the symptoms of asthma,

---

[80] *Out West*, Volume I, No. 7, May 16, 1872.

[81] *Out West*, Volume I, No. 7, May 16, 1872. For much the same reason, some modern athletes choose to train at high altitude because the increased lung strength from exercise at altitude requires gives them a physical advantage over athletes who train at lower altitudes.

[82] Ibid.

[83] Abbot, Leonard, and Noel, *Colorado: A History of the Centennial State*, 228.

bronchitis, and other respiratory ailments for as long as they remained in the dry climate.[84] By the 1840s, physicians proposing treatments for tuberculosis were emphasizing the benefits of cold alpine winter air because of its dryness and purity.[85] Those afflicted with consumption (and those misdiagnosed with it) began immigrating in massive numbers to the dry mountain climate Colorado offered as soon as it was easy to reach by train. Beyond just the "lungers," as TB patients were often called, people suffering from asthma, dyspepsia, nervous exhaustion, and other infirmities travelled across the plains seeking the pure Colorado air.[86] The promise of clean and dry air filled the Colorado-bound trains with health seekers.

Boosters also promised sunshine in what probably seemed like ridiculous amounts to potential immigrants. Newcomers to Colorado marveled at the fact that "three-fourths, at least, of the days, are perfectly cloudless," and that sunny days were not at all uncommon even through the winter.[87] Newspapers hastened to add that not all days were bright and pleasant, but so many cloudless days made for a great improvement just in the cheerfulness of invalids, not to mention the many important physical benefits of sunshine for those suffering from a vast range of infirmities. Even if Colorado was not quite as sunny as the promoters promised, it was certainly sunnier through the fall and winter months than most states in the East. A TB patient or other invalid instructed to get as much sun as possible could find plenty of it in Colorado in every month of the year.

Whatever ailment caused Elsie W. Chambers' delicacy, it seemed that Colorado might just hold the cure—or at least some relief, if it was asthma or something of

---

[84] *Out West*, Volume I, No. 25, September 19, 1872. We speculate that Mrs. Chambers suffered from asthma or some other respiratory ailment.

[85] Daniel, *Captain of Death*, 168.

[86] Abbott, Leonard, and Noel, 229.

[87] *Out West*, Volume I, No. 7, May 16, 1872.

the like that plagued her. Furthermore, how could a hardworking farming family resist one Colorado booster's call that

> …the prudent and industrious can here often better their fortunes financially, and can certainly gain an honest livelihood, while the best of tonics and stimulants— this dry, pure, mountain air—repairs the wastes of disease, and gives vigor for years of useful, joyous service for God and humanity.[88]

The *Out West* and many other editorials made the case that the restored health Colorado could bestow would enable the once-sickly to better serve God and their fellow men—an argument that, in the case of the Chambers, proved correct. Thus, seeking better health for Elsie, the Chambers prepared to move west to see if the famous Colorado climate would do all that the boosters and their friends said it could.

With some preparation, the Chambers family was well set up to make a successful move to Colorado. Before 1874, Robert Chambers had been a successful wheat farmer in southern Wisconsin and then on the ancestral Chambers-Barber family farm in Limestone Township, Pennsylvania. The 1870 census lists Robert as a farmer living with his father, Benjamin, his younger sister, Henrietta, his great aunt, Eleanor Barber, and his two-year-old son, Benjamin.[89]

Figure 6 - 1870 census. Robert Chambers in household of Benjamin Chambers.

He continued to farm in Limestone after he and Elsie Woolsey married in 1871, and their daughter Eleanor was born in April 1873. After a productive wheat crop

---

[88] *Out West*, Volume I, No. 34, December 5, 1872.

[89] "United States Census, 1870", database with images, Robert Chambers in entry for Benjamin Chambers, 1870. Benjamin was born in September 1867 to Robert Chambers and his first wife, Mary Lockart, while they were living in Wisconsin near Robert's other siblings. After Mary died, Robert, his father Ben, and his son Ben moved back to the family farm in Limestone, where his sister Henrietta took care of baby Ben.

and the sale of the farm and livestock in the spring of 1874, Robert Chambers had $10,000 in cash with which to start west—the equivalent of $232,000 in 2020 dollars.[90] The Chambers were by no means poor homesteaders or penniless invalids with nothing to their name. They were well-equipped to set themselves up successfully in Colorado.

There was no single train that could carry the Chambers from Limestone to Denver, where they initially intended to settle. The family would have to travel on at least five different railroad lines to reach their destination. For the first leg of their journey from Pennsylvania, Robert's sister Henrietta (often called Nettie) rode along with Robert, Ben, Eleanor, and Elsie, who was expecting another child. Nettie had helped to take care of young Ben Chambers since Robert Chambers' first wife, Mary, died. She had remained with the Chambers at their farm in Pennsylvania after Robert married Elsie in 1871. When Robert Chambers sold the Limestone farm and moved west, however, it was decided that it would be best for Nettie to move back to Monroe, Wisconsin, to live with the rest of the Chambers siblings instead of travelling all the way to the "terrible far west."[91] Thus, the first train ride was from Pennsylvania to the Chambers siblings' farms in southern Wisconsin, where Nettie would stay with her older siblings: Eleanor "Nellie" Chambers Stair, John Chambers, and Mary Chambers Stair.[92] For a brief time, all five siblings were reunited. The record of this visit is preserved in a photograph of the five Chambers siblings that is dated April 1874 (see Figure 7).

---

[90] Mary Chambers DeLong, "The Chambers Family History," 1. Some Chambers family oral histories record that Robert Chambers had also raised cattle in Wisconsin during the Civil War—he was not accepted to fight in the war because he had been injured in the knee with an axe and always limped for the rest of his life. Instead of fighting he stayed home and farmed with his father, and according to some family histories earned significant income raising and selling cattle (Recollections of Dorothy Chambers, wife of Robert Chambers II).

[91] Mary Chambers Delong, "Chambers Family History," 3.

[92] Ibid., 2. Mary wrote that the Wisconsin Chambers lived near Monroe and Brodlead, Wisconsin.

44

Figure 7 - Chambers siblings April 1874: Mary C. Stair, Eleanor C. Stair, Henrietta (Nettie) Chambers, Robert Chambers, John Chambers. Courtesy Bruce W. Dunbar Family Collection.

From Wisconsin, the Chambers began their journey to Colorado in earnest. They first travelled southwest through Iowa and eventually connected with the Union Pacific Railroad, which they rode to Cheyenne, Wyoming. Mary Chambers DeLong writes that Robert Chambers carried his $10,000 in cash rolled up in his pocket the whole way from Pennsylvania to Colorado, "with just a tiny pistol not more than 8 inches long including the handle" to protect the money and the family.[93] Any time he had to pay for anything, Robert would pull out the wad of cash, which his family described as "big enough to choke a horse," and count out what was necessary. His daughter later recounted that Elsie seethed at this, worried that this reckless behavior would result in harm to him, herself, or the children.[94] Nonetheless, the family—children, cash, and all—arrived in Denver safely. The pistol remained unfired.

[93] Mary Chambers DeLong, "The Chambers Family History," 1.

[94] Ibid.

What did not remain intact on the train to Denver, however, were the family's plans to settle there. On the train between Cheyenne and Denver, a fellow passenger and Colorado booster James Wolfe, a director of El Paso County Bank in Colorado Springs, sang the praises of Colorado Springs to Robert Chambers and convinced him to make the extra trip south to see it. Robert made a three-day journey down to Colorado Springs and apparently fell in love with it—something that he, with his wad of cash, could afford to do.[95] Colorado Springs was no haven for the penniless. Rental housing costs in Colorado in general were higher than in the East by fifteen percent, and Colorado Springs was the most expensive place to live in the state.[96] It was the ideal resort for the rich and famous from the East to come and recover in luxury. Those who arrived poor, however, often barely survived in tent cities because they could find neither a cheap enough place to stay nor work that would not compromise their health. The Chambers fit into neither of these camps, for they did have enough money to wait and see if the climate would help. If it did, they would establish themselves in Colorado's most expensive resort town. Robert found temporary lodging in Colorado Springs and brought Elsie, Ben, and Eleanor down to join him. He purchased a piece of property on the corner of Monument and Weber, with an unfinished house on it, which he completed swiftly. Elsie gave birth to her second daughter, Bessie, in that house in Colorado Springs on June 15th, 1874.

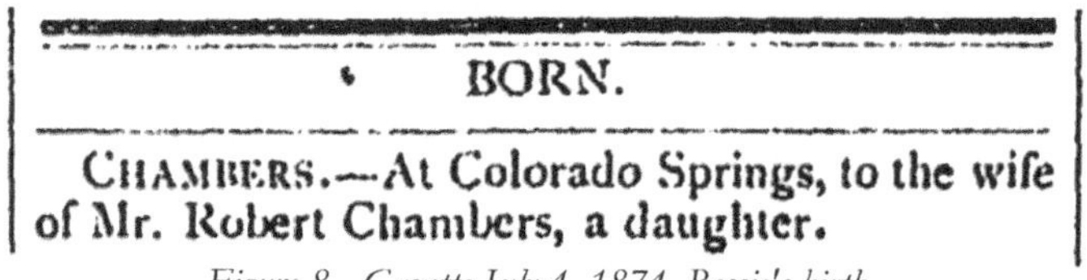

BORN.

CHAMBERS.—At Colorado Springs, to the wife of Mr. Robert Chambers, a daughter.

Figure 8 - Gazette July 4, 1874. Bessie's birth.

---

[95] Mary Chambers DeLong, "The Chambers Family History," 1.

[96] Andrew Gulliford, "Come Only if Rich: The health-seeker movement in Colorado Springs," Collection CU 83. Special Collections, Pikes Peak Library District, 4.

Now the family had only to "await the effects of the climate," as Elsie W. Chambers herself described.[97] Thankfully, they did not have to wait for long. Elsie wrote later that "by fall [her] health was so far improved that he [Robert] determined to remain in Colorado."[98] The Colorado climate had made its move fast, and Elsie was well again. For the Chambers, the promises made by newspapers and friends about the wonders of Colorado's clean, high, and dry air had come true. There are no written records of Elsie ever experiencing any relapse, and the records of her busy life in Colorado Springs in the years to come certainly imply that she was no invalid. Her symptoms were cured or significantly relieved by the Colorado climate. Sadly, Elsie's newborn baby girl was not as healthy. Young Bessie Chambers only lived four months, and the *Colorado Springs Gazette*

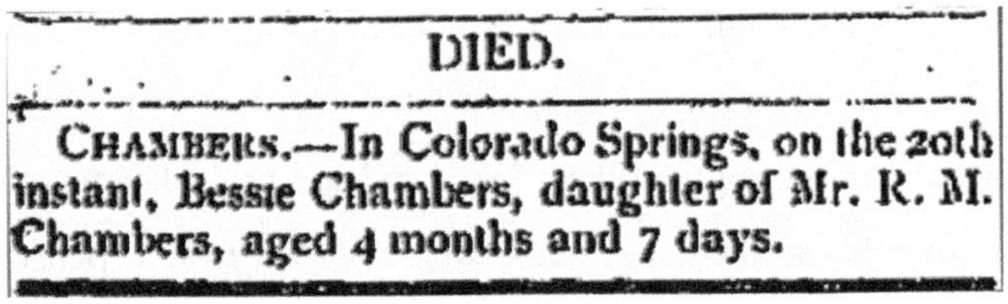

DIED.

CHAMBERS.—In Colorado Springs, on the 20th instant, Bessie Chambers, daughter of Mr. R. M. Chambers, aged 4 months and 7 days.

Figure 9 - Gazette October 24, 1874. Bessie's death.

records Bessie's death on October 24th, 1874. The loss of a child was an experience many families at this time could empathize with, because the mortality rate of children under five was around thirty percent in America in the 1870s.[99] Bessie Chambers was one of the earliest burials in Mount Washington Cemetery (now Evergreen Cemetery), which was established in 1874.

Meanwhile, Robert Chambers had found their new home, a homestead claim just east of the Garden of the Gods. About four miles from Colorado Springs proper, it had the crucial factor necessary for any kind of successful farming in Colorado: water rights. Robert Chambers paid the owner, Walter Galloway, $1,400 for the one hundred and sixty acres in November 1874—the equivalent of $32,500 in today's money—and in early 1875 paid carpenter Joseph Leighton $300 to

---

[97] Elsie Woolsey Chambers, "What Happened While the Cabin Lived," 5.

[98] Ibid., 5.

[99] Gretchen A. Gondran, "Declining Mortality in the United States in the Late Nineteenth and Early Twentieth Centuries," *Annales de Démographie Historique,* 1987.

construct a small wood frame house on it.[100] In February, Robert, Elsie, and their two children moved out of their house in town and into the small frame house that would later become the kitchen of the enlarged stone farmhouse. They waited here for the rest of the house to be completed. The size of this small kitchen is another proof of Elsie's thorough recovery—this was no luxury house, but a bare bones little frame building that was, no doubt, a cold room in which to live in February. Elsie named the farm Rock Ledge Ranch, and the rest of the farmhouse was built with locally quarried stone that displayed the same lovely tan, orange, and red hues of the Garden of the Gods sandstone.[101]

By mid-June 1875, the Rock Ledge House was finished and livable. The *Colorado Springs Gazette* reported on June 19th that not only was the "handsome stone

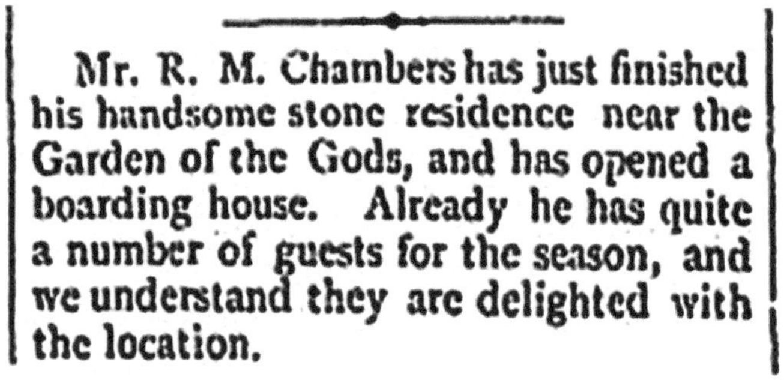

> **Mr. R. M. Chambers has just finished his handsome stone residence near the Garden of the Gods, and has opened a boarding house. Already he has quite a number of guests for the season, and we understand they are delighted with the location.**

Figure 10 - Gazette June 19, 1875. Rock Ledge House completed and open for boarders.

residence" completed, but that the Chambers family was already renting out rooms to boarders. A week later, the *Gazette* mentioned their boarders by name, stating, "Among those stopping with Mr. Chambers, at his private boarding house in the Garden of the Gods, are Lewis Rultkay and family and Mrs. Collins, of Des Moines, Iowa."[102] Clearly the Colorado climate had done wonders for Elsie—

---

[100] Elsie Woolsey Chambers, "What Happened While the Cabin Lived," 5, and Carol Kennis Lopez, "Agricultural Legacy: Rock Ledge Ranch Historic Site," 6. $300 in 1874 is worth nearly $7,000 in today's money.

[101] Mary Chambers DeLong, "The Chambers Family History," 1. Writings by Mary Chambers DeLong state that the builders "[got] the stone from the quarry on the land," but it remains uncertain whether that means they quarried the stone from Rock Ledge Ranch property or from any of the local quarries (of which there are several within reasonable distance with the same type of stone).

[102] *Colorado Springs Gazette,* June 26, 1875.

48

because now, though once again expecting a baby, she was running a boarding house!

Builders completed the Rock Ledge House just in time for the Chambers' youngest daughter, Mary, to be born in the master bedroom on the first floor. Apparently this was due in no small part to the insistence of Mrs. Chambers: Mary Chambers DeLong wrote that "Mother kept urging them to hurry as she wanted me to be born in the new house."[103] She wrote that the house was "finished enough" that Mary Chambers was born in Mrs. Chambers' bedroom on August 20, 1875.[104] Caring for a new baby and providing for boarders once again shows that Elsie W. Chambers was clearly no longer suffering ill health. The picture of the family on the following page (Figure 11) was taken four years later, in 1879.

[103] Mary Chambers Delong, "Chambers Family History," 3.

[104] Ibid., 3.

Figure 11 - The Chambers Family, 1879. From left to right: Eleanor, Elsie, Ben, Robert, Mary.
Courtesy Bruce W. Dunbar Family Collection.

The house, indeed handsome and about two thousand square feet in total, was an ideal boarding place for tourists and health seekers, as well as for maintaining the health of the family.[105] The thick stone walls insulated the house remarkably well and continue to do so to this day, keeping out the heat on even the hottest summer days and keeping in the heat during the winter. Large windows in every room let in plenty of the Colorado sunlight that was supposed to do wonders for invalids. On both the first and second floor, the front room windows also serve as French doors that open out onto the large front porches, enabling the family and any visitors to obey their doctors and spend hours out in the pure Colorado air soaking up the sun. Abundant natural light is a great strength of the house, and the Chambers capitalized on it by keeping the inside of the house light and airy as well. A century later, as the Rock Ledge House underwent extensive restorations, wallpaper scraps found in the walls revealed the colors and patterns chosen by the Chambers. These scarps show the Chambers' disregard of current styles in favor of Mrs. Chambers' preferences and a bright house. Rather than decorating their home with the dark and garish styles typical of Victorian wallpaper, the Chambers chose lighter colors, including yellow in all five of the bedrooms (one on the first floor and four upstairs).

Clearly the Chambers were not blind to the opportunities their new home presented. They knew that people like themselves were flocking to Colorado Springs in search of health and would need places to stay, just like they had. Spotting an additional means of income, they took the chance. It is likely that the idea of renting out rooms to boarders occurred to the Chambers even before they built their home, for the Rock Ledge House contains many features that made it work exceedingly well as a boarding house. A back staircase from the kitchen would enable someone to reach the bedrooms upstairs without walking through the rest of the house to the front staircase. The house contains more doors than appears reasonable at first—until one considers the fact that the family took in

---

[105] I am not the first to note that the Rock Ledge House is well set up to house TB patients. Former Rock Ledge Ranch Manager, Carol Kennis Lopez, commented on this idea in the Rock Ledge House training manual she composed, in reference to the windows of the house.

boarders. If a room was occupied, there was always another way to move to a different room without disturbing the occupants. The dining room, which contains two closets as well as doors that lead directly outside, could be split into two separate dining rooms by massive double doors in the center. This enabled the family to serve meals at different times or to eat separately from their guests. Alternatively, they could leave the doors open and eat in one big room. There is even a tiny hallway under the stairs that made it possible for family members or boarders to move from the dining room nearer the kitchen to the front hall without traipsing through the smaller half of the dining room. No space in the house is wasted. It appears that the Chambers thought of everything.

Both the design and the location of the Chambers' new farmhouse was ideal for both tourists and health seekers. Rock Ledge Ranch lies just southeast of the gateway to the Garden of the Gods, one of the most popular tourist destinations in the state both then and now. Between beautiful views and touring convenience, the Chambers' home clearly provided the perfect place to stay for those seeking scenic views and mild adventure in Colorado Springs. Yet the Rock Ledge House was also the temporary home of invalids who, like Mrs. Chambers herself, were hoping and praying the Colorado air would do as much good as the boosters swore it would. It is very reasonable to assume that some of the Chambers' boarders would have been health seekers, and family histories indicate that they were. Mary Chambers DeLong wrote that many of the boarders were "T.B.ers from the East," and indicated that the family hosted boarders mainly in the summers.[106] Boarding invalids was not just an accident, however.

The Chambers purposefully advertised for invalid boarders at Rock Ledge Ranch. From 1875 on through the end of the decade, the Chambers regularly placed ads for boarders in the *Colorado Springs Gazette*. An ad first appearing in the paper on August 28, 1875, specifically advertises for both invalids and tourists. This advertisement appears in the *Gazette* every two weeks for the months of

---

[106] Mary Chambers Delong, "Chambers Family History," 2.

August and September. Robert Chambers was not only a farmer. He was an entrepreneur. He knew firsthand that many of the people moving to Colorado—either for the season or permanently—were health seekers, and he purposed to make a profit from the business they brought to the region. The Chambers offered a private home in a beautiful location, near Colorado Springs but outside of the city itself, to those desiring to stay days, weeks, or months.

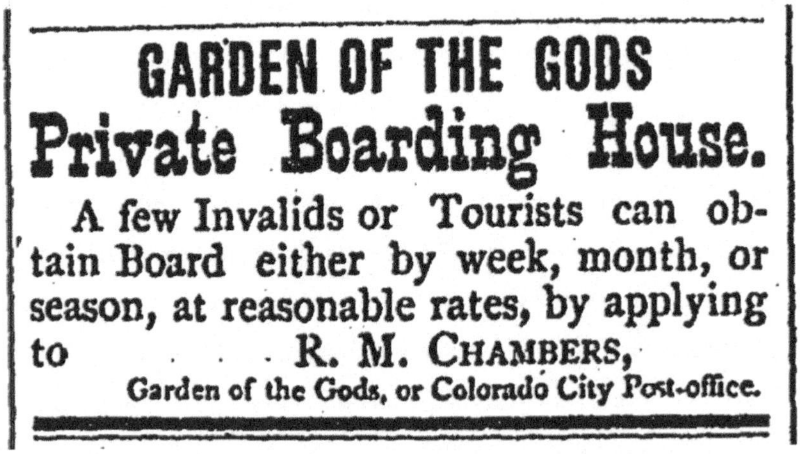

GARDEN OF THE GODS
Private Boarding House.

A few Invalids or Tourists can obtain Board either by week, month, or season, at reasonable rates, by applying to   . . . R. M. CHAMBERS,
Garden of the Gods, or Colorado City Post-office.

Figure 12 - Gazette August 28, 1875. Ad for "Invalids or Tourists."

The fact that this ad ran in the paper in September implies that the Chambers took in boarders beyond just the summer months. Indeed, Colorado tourism and health-seeking typically came in different seasons. During the summer, Colorado Springs was a mountain resort for hundreds of tourists who visited to enjoy the scenery and explore the great outdoors. Once they vacated their hotels and boarding houses come autumn, health seekers trying to escape the damp and dark Eastern winters took their place. Colorado Springs, which is sunny for over three hundred days a year and delivers mild days even in the middle of winter, was considered an excellent place for invalids through the cold months.[107] The Chambers understood this cycle of visitors, which is evident in their advertising. Their summer and early fall advertisements are aimed at both the infirm and the

---

[107] Abbot, Leonard, and Noel, *Colorado: A History of the Centennial State*, 229.

vacationers, while those later in the year are clearly more directed at invalids. An advertisement placed in a regional newspaper in December of 1876 proclaims that the Chambers would pay "special attention" to the needs of their invalid guests.[108] Family history indicates that the Rock Ledge House was often full of boarders, and the Chambers kept this business running from the house for many years. They had found an additional income stream that worked for them, and they continued it throughout the late 1800s as "lungers" and other invalids streamed into Colorado.

Figure 13 - Advertisement in the Colorado Mountaineer, December 20, 1876--note the existence of an ad placed during the winter!

The cost of boarding at Rock Ledge Ranch was less expensive than many other places in Colorado Springs at the time—but that does not mean it was cheap. Rock Ledge Ranch ads in the papers in April 1876 reveal that boarding at the Ranch cost $1.50 a night or anywhere from $6 to $9 per week—which would be about $140 to $220 in 2020 dollars. This was much more expensive than boarding back East, but it was on the lower end of the spectrum for boarding in Colorado Springs at this time, where rooms might cost as much $25 a week.[109] Still, $6 per week was no

---

[108] *The Colorado Mountaineer,* December 20, 1876.

[109] Andrew Gulliford, "Come Only if Rich: The health-seeker movement in Colorado Springs," 5. This would be the equivalent of $600 per week in 2020 dollars.

easy price to pay. Many men at this time earned only a dollar a day, and Colorado Springs housekeeping jobs for women paid $5 a week.[110] The Chambers' boarders would have had to be fairly well-off to afford room and board in the Rock Ledge House.

SPECIAL NOTICES.

BOARDING,

From $6 to $9 per week, at Rock Ledge Ranch, near the Garden of the Gods.

Figure 14 - Gazette April 1, 1876. Boarding prices at Rock Ledge Ranch.

Taking sick strangers into one's house is an idea totally foreign to the modern mind. Were the Chambers not concerned about their children being infected with tuberculosis from their boarders? There are many facets to the answer. First, it is undeniable that the Chambers advertised for invalid boarders, so clearly it was not enough of a concern to deter them. No written records indicate concern that sick boarders would make the children or Mrs. Chambers ill. Perhaps this communicates great confidence in Colorado's climate cure. The family had seen the climate's successful effect on Mrs. Chambers, so it is not unreasonable to speculate that they would have taken comfort in that. Yet another important point to remember is that in 1875 myths and misinformation about tuberculosis persisted among doctors and laypeople. People did not understand how contagious the disease was, and this may be another reason why the Chambers were not concerned.

From what is known of the Chambers, it seems that a spirit of generosity as well as entrepreneurship motivated their housing of the sick. They were active members of their church and community, and the stories told about them indicate that they were hospitable as well as enterprising. One example is recorded in "What Happened While the Cabin Lived," a brief account of Rock Ledge Ranch

---

[110] Gulliford, 5.

written by Elsie W. Chambers herself. In it, Mrs. Chambers tells the charming story of the Chambers providing shelter to a man bringing his ill son down to Colorado Springs from the mountains:

> Santa Claus horses were probably the largest oxen ever known in Colorado. Their owner was bringing his invalid son down from the mountains, and night overtaking him, he was lost in the Garden of the Gods and stopped over night. The children were told the oxen were Santa Claus's horses and only knew oxen by that name for some time.[111]

Apparently on at least some occasions, the Chambers' hosting of invalids was out of generosity and charity, not just for the sake of making money. For whatever reason, the risk of contracting whatever illnesses their guests had did not seem to bother them.

Perhaps another reason the Chambers did not express concern about having consumptives in their home was the fact that Colorado Springs was full of "lungers." TB patients began to fill Colorado Springs hotels and boarding houses as soon as train travel made the trip more possible for the ill. By June 1873, there were enough consumptives around town that a group of nuns suggested a sanatorium for those trying to recover from the disease.[112] In the next twenty-five years, over a dozen sanatoriums sprang up across the city. In many places, these sanatoriums housed patients in "Gardiner tents," which were octagonal canvas tents designed by Colorado Springs doctor Charles Fox Gardiner that allowed consumptives to spend as much time in the open air as possible.[113] At the nicer

---

[111] Elsie Woolsey Chambers, "What Happened While the Cabin Lived," 5-6.

[112] Gulliford, 2, and Loe, 27.

[113] Loe, 35.

56

Figure 15 - Woman outside TB hut. From the collection of the Colorado Springs Pioneers Museum.

Figure 16 - TB patients sit outside huts at Woodmen Sanatorium in the snow. From the collection of the Colorado Springs Pioneers Museum.

sanitoriums, these temporary tents were eventually replaced by more permanent structures of similar size and purpose. Sanatoriums contained rows upon rows of tiny octagonal huts with tall, pointed roofs, each containing one TBer who would spend as much of his day as possible outside soaking up the sun and the fresh dry air.[114]

Eventually, Dr. Samuel Edwin Solly, a friend of General Palmer and a former consumptive himself, planned and founded the most famous of these sanatoriums. He had spent years promoting Colorado Springs as the best place in the world for TB patients, writing extensively about the nearly miraculous cure that consumptives could experience in the "Sunshine City."[115] Solly was originally from England himself, and due to his influence many immigrants came to Colorado from England in the early years of the city. By 1885, nearly nine hundred

---

[114] Gulliford, 2. These TB huts can still be found in odd places around Colorado Springs and Manitou—one was moved to Rock Ledge Ranch and now serves as the admissions hut for the site.

[115] Abbott, Leonard, and Noel, *Colorado: A History of the Centennial State*, 229.

English-born citizens made up about ten percent of the population of Colorado Springs.[116] For former inhabitants of cloudy England, the Colorado sunshine was undoubtedly a strikingly different climate.

Swarms of consumptives flocked to Colorado and Colorado Springs in particular. Sanatoriums, hotels, and boarding houses were full of "lungers," the city was full of doctors serving the sick, and Colorado Springs papers were full of advertisements for pills and powders that promised to "positively cure!" tuberculosis. It is impossible to know how many individuals suffering from tuberculosis came to Colorado Springs, but it was easily in the tens of thousands.[117] What can be measured is the population in Colorado Springs during these years, which grew from 3,000 in 1874, to 11,000 in 1890, to 21,000 in 1900.[118] While this growth was not as dramatic as that of Denver, which saw its population skyrocket from nearly 5,000 in 1870 to over 130,000 in 1900, this is because of the seasonal health seekers.[119] Colorado Springs more often gained the business of wealthy but sickly vacationers coming to stay for the season rather than for good. There was certainly plenty of room for them: by 1878, Colorado Springs could house 25,000 guests in hotels and boardinghouses, and sanatoriums were springing up quickly as well.[120] Dependent on health seekers, many Colorado Springs businessmen purchased advertising in the East to bring more sickly sojourners to their town.[121] The Chambers were not alone in capitalizing on this opportunity to make a living by caring for the many rich consumptives seeking lodging in the region.

For years, Colorado Springs emphasized and celebrated its identity as the Sunshine City—"a beautiful home for an invalid" —but that began to end in the

---

[116] Loe, 39.

[117] Ibid., 230.

[118] "Population of Colorado Springs, CO." Population.us, https://population.us/co/colorado-springs/

[119] "Population of Denver, CO," Population.us, https://population.us/co/denver/

[120] Abbott, Leonard, and Noel, *Colorado: A History of the Centennial State*, 227.

[121] Gulliford, 3.

late 1880s and 1890s.[122] As people began to understand more about tuberculosis and how it was spread, they grew more concerned. City ordinances in the mid to late 1880s required that individuals with infectious diseases be reported by doctors and labelled at their lodging places, and by the 1890s tuberculosis was added to that list of diseases that must be reported.[123] As the percentage of deaths due to tuberculosis rose, so did the alarm about its spread, and cities began to fear that the health-seeking immigrants were infecting their healthy citizens. In 1897, city ordinances began to require boarding houses and hotels to report invalid guests. The period of quarantining and cleaning the guest's room meant that boarding houses could lose money by taking in TB patients, for it would prevent them from taking in more guests.[124] What had once been a money-making opportunity was now a liability for Colorado Springs hotels and boarding houses. This may have affected the Chambers family and perhaps caused them to stop taking in TB patients, as the added laws about invalid boarders meant such guests constituted more of a risk than a benefit to a family's constitutions and finances. By 1900, "lungers" faced a negative social stigma as well as difficulty in finding lodging. The disease that had made Colorado Springs famous became an anathema, something to be concealed. Only the very rich could afford to seek the climate cure, and even then in much secrecy.

Of course, tuberculosis patients were probably not the only kind of invalid that stayed with the Chambers, because "lungers" were not the only health seekers in Colorado Springs. Technically located in Colorado City, Rock Ledge Ranch was just a few miles from Manitou Springs, which, unlike Colorado Springs, was true to its name: it offered springs. In addition to all the climate cure benefits that Colorado Springs had to offer, Manitou Springs boasted mineral water that came up in springs throughout the small town. Alongside many other physicians, Dr.

---

[122] *Out West*, Volume I, No. 25, September 19, 1872.

[123] Gulliford, 6.

[124] Ibid., 8.

S.E. Solly declared that the mineral waters were beneficial for the blood and the digestive system.[125] Resorts quickly sprung up throughout this small town, and hotel rooms filled swiftly. People flocked from all across the nation to experience the benefits of the increasingly popular water cure—and the Chambers could offer nearby lodging for those who sought the benefits of the mineral waters.

The water cure, or hydropathy, had been around for hundreds of years, but it was taking America by storm in the 1870s as increased opportunities for travel meant more and more people could visit springs and spas. The water cure had two facets—drinking mineral water and bathing in it—which could be taken individually or together.[126] Exercise was also an important part of the treatment: a day of the water cure meant walking from spring to spring drinking the waters.[127] One theory behind hydropathy was that in soaking in water, the body would exchange the impurities within itself for the nutrients in the water.[128] Drinking the mineral water was, by this theory, an equally effective way to get the beneficial minerals into one's system. American hydropathy resorts were often placed in scenic rural locations in order to provide patients with a healthy refuge of peace and rest.

Manitou was no exception. People seeking cures to all sorts of ailments ("from alcoholism to lunacy to warts") came to Manitou for the mineral waters, as many middle-class Americans became obsessed with the water cure in the mid-1800s.[129] By 1883, those guests could enjoy the comforts of the elegant Manitou bathhouse. They had their choice of hot or cold, Russian vapor, or electric baths.[130] Then, dressed in their best, these wealthy health seekers would stroll from spring to

[125] Abbott, Noel, and Leonard, *Colorado: A History of the Centennial State*, 229.

[126] Kathryn Kish Sklar, "All Hail to Pure Cold Water!" (*American Heritage* 26, no. 1, 1974), 2.

[127] Loe, 27.

[128] James C. Whorton, *Nature Cures: The History of Alternative Medicine in America* (Oxford: Oxford University Press, 2002), 83.

[129] Loe, 33.

[130] Ibid., 30.

60

spring throughout the resort town, gaining strength from the sun and the exercise as well as the mineral waters. Manitou became famous across the United States. By the 1880s about two thousand health seekers were visiting the small resort town every summer hoping for healing and restoration.[131] Some of them probably stayed in the "handsome stone residence" at Rock Ledge Ranch while visiting the mineral waters.

While it is unknown what kind of invalids found respite at Rock Ledge Ranch, the Chambers family willingly took in the sick and the well for at least two decades while they lived in Colorado Springs. Newspaper ads for boarders continue to appear in newspapers throughout the 1870s, and a family photo taken in front of the house in the 1880s includes two individuals identified as boarders sitting on the porch as the family stands off to the side in front of the house.

Figure 17 - The Rock Ledge House, approximately 1880. Eleanor is holding the horse (a gift from Aunt Nettie) while Mary sits on it. Robert and Elsie stand just behind. On the porch sit two individuals identified as boarders. Courtesy Bruce W. Dunbar Family Collection.

---

[131] Loe, 30.

Boarding brought society as well as income to the Chambers family: in 1891 Ben Chambers married Madge Kinney, who according to family records had boarded with the Chambers.[132] Family histories recount the story that because the family continued to take in boarders, Ben and Madge lived outside in a tent, and their first son to live past infancy, Robert Chambers II, was born in that tent on June 17th, 1895.[133] Throughout their time in Colorado Springs, the Chambers made excellent use of their location and beautiful home by offering space to visitors of all kinds, a regular business for their family.

From their very reason for moving west to one of their streams of income, the Chambers' story lines up with one of the largest themes in pre-1900 Colorado Springs. Illness brought business. Because they came with enough money to stay and establish themselves well, the Chambers saw beneficial results from the climate that the boosters had praised to the sunny Colorado skies. Even once Mrs. Chambers had recovered, the Chambers' story exemplifies that the economy of Colorado Springs in the last quarter of the nineteenth century relied on the business of these incoming health seekers. At first, the health seekers meant good business for everyone. The railroad brought them, hotels and restaurants housed and fed them, doctors cured them, and farmers provided food for them. Colorado Springs developed because of the massive influx of water cure fanatics and coughing consumptives. These health seekers provided a crucial source of revenue for Colorado Springs residents like the Chambers. It would prove absolutely necessary in years when agriculture could not be depended on—as was, unfortunately, the case in the first several years of Rock Ledge Ranch.

---

[132] Dorothy Chambers, "The Ben Chambers Family Still Lives in Colorado," 2, and *Colorado Springs Gazette*, August 29, 1891.

[133] Dorothy Chambers, "The Ben Chambers Family Still Lives in Colorado," 2, and *Colorado Springs Gazette,* June 22, 1895.

Chapter Three

"Patient Persistent Effort:"
Thriving Agriculturally at Rock Ledge Ranch

The boosters had promised that the western climate could provide a cure for the sick, and for the Chambers and many others, Colorado made good on that promise. Would it also supply their needs for making a living? The Chambers were experienced farmers, but Colorado and the West proved a challenge for many who had been competent agriculturalists back East. Despite seasons of dryness and plagues of locusts, between 1874 and 1900 Rock Ledge Ranch became a remarkable success due to the ingenuity and perseverance of the Chambers family and their practice of agricultural diversification. Tracing the obstacles the Chambers faced—and how they overcame them—tells not just their story, but also the broader story of Colorado agriculture in the last quarter of the nineteenth century.

Even before the Chambers arrived, the property that became Rock Ledge Ranch was involved in one of the most important stories of the settlement of the West: homesteading. During the Civil War, Congress passed the Homestead Act, which allowed for heads of households (or single adults) to claim 160 acres of federal land. There was no price, only the requirement that they live on it and improve it for five years. Why did this bill come through when it did? Republicans

64

had pushed for the Homestead Act in the 1850s as a way to ensure the West filled
with small family farms, not slave-operated plantations. The territories out West
would then become free states, so that one day free states would outnumber slave
states.[134] Ideally, the Homestead Act would first prevent the spread of slavery and
then hopefully help to end it. The South, however, saw through this plan and
blocked the Homestead Act in Congress throughout the 1850s, thus it did not pass
Congress until the middle of the Civil War. On January 1, 1863—the same day as
the Emancipation Proclamation—the Homestead Act became law.

In the 123 years the Homestead Act remained in effect, four million homestead
claims were filed as millions of Americans and immigrants settled in the West.
Among these pioneers was Walter Galloway, a Scottish immigrant and Civil War
veteran who came to Colorado in 1866. At that point, the area including the future
Rock Ledge Ranch had not yet been surveyed, so Galloway was unable to register
an official homestead claim on the land he intended to farm. Nonetheless, he lived
(or "squatted") next to Camp Creek and Garden of the Gods from 1867 until
1871, as both Elsie W. Chambers' writings and El Paso County tax records
attest.[135] Once the land was surveyed in 1871, Galloway was able to legalize his
homestead claim to the 160 acres southeast of the gateway to the Garden of the
Gods.[136] In the years he lived on the ranch property, Galloway worked as a day
laborer and constructed a cabin, which was later used by the Chambers as a stable
and eventually torn down.[137]

Because he had not been able to register his homestead claim in 1867, Galloway
did not yet own the land when Robert Chambers offered to purchase it from him
in 1874. To fulfill the stipulations of the Homestead Act, Galloway owed the

[134] Brands, *Dreams of El Dorado,* 287-288.

[135] Elsie Chambers, "What Happened While the Cabin Lived," 1, and Carol Kennis Lopez, "Agricultural Legacy: Rock Ledge Ranch Historic Site" (Unpublished manuscript, 2017), 5.

[136] This property is described in the legal documents as "Southeast quarter of section 34 in township 13 south of range 67 west in the 6th Principal Meridian, containing 160 acres." Lopez, 5, and Galloway Deed.

[137] Elsie Chambers, "What Happened While the Cabin Lived," 5.

government at least two more years of living on the land before it lawfully became his. But the act also contained provisions for situations such as these. If a homesteader had lived on the land for at least a year, he could purchase it for $1.25 an acre ($29 an acre in 2020 dollars). Robert Chambers, with his wad of cash in his pocket, was more than willing to pay Galloway's "fee for proving up" as well as the $1400 for the land itself.[138] Thus on November 9th, 1874, Galloway purchased his homestead for the sum of $200 (about $4,600 in 2020). Chambers had provided the cash so that Galloway could buy out the claim.

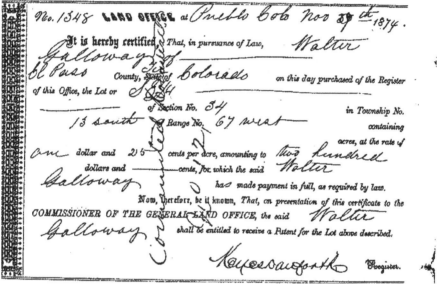

Figure 18 - November 9, 1874. Land Office receipt for Galloway's purchase of Rock Ledge Ranch property. (Rock Ledge Ranch Historic Site)

The very next day, November 10th, Galloway sold the property to Chambers for $1400 ($32,500 in 2020).

---

[138] Elsie Chambers, "What Happened While the Cabin Lived," 1.

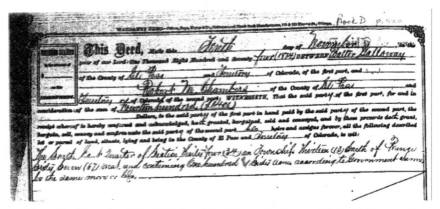

Figure 19 - November 10th, 1874. Land deed/transaction between Walter Galloway and Robert Chambers. (Rock Ledge Ranch Historic Site)

Elsie W. Chambers wrote that Galloway "felt that he was well paid, and that he could go home quite a rich man. Nothing has been heard from him since his return to his eastern house."[139] Though only lawfully a homestead for three years, Rock Ledge Ranch demonstrates multiple facets of the Homestead Act that made settlement of the West possible.

Robert Chambers now had his ranch; what would he do with it? Writings by later descendants and family members imply or explicitly state that Chambers was looking for "a good place for a fruit ranch, with ample water" when he came to Colorado.[140] What could have motivated this? Family histories record that Robert Chambers had mostly grown wheat and also raised livestock in Pennsylvania and Wisconsin, but Elsie had grown up on a fruit orchard in Lloyd, New York, which is in the Hudson River Valley.[141] Whether their original intent was fruit or not, the Chambers succeeded in finding a farm that could sustain the agricultural projects they would take on in the years to come. Before they could get their feet under them, however, in flew the grasshoppers.

---

[139] Elsie Chambers, "What Happened While the Cabin Lived," 1.

[140] Mary Chambers DeLong, "The Chambers Family History" 3, and Grace DeLong, "A Ranch Begins: The Chambers Period 1874-1900," 3.

[141] Mary Chambers DeLong, "The Chambers Family History," 2.

While Elsie Chambers gives the grasshoppers only a passing mention in her account "What Happened While the Cabin Lived," her descendants devote a few more words to the pests that plagued Colorado in the mid-1870s.[142] Mary Chambers DeLong, the Chambers' younger daughter who was born in the Rock Ledge House, wrote of the early years of the ranch:

> There was also much tough going for Father. First, the terrible scourge of grasshoppers which lasted for three years all over the Middlewest. On account of this, he bought milk cows and ran a dairy. The grasshoppers devoured every spear of green and he had to buy feed for the cows.[143]

All the cash in the world could not drive away the grasshoppers. Property with ample water was necessary for farming, but if the grasshoppers ate everything that grew, it would do little good for the Chambers family. They would need something besides plans for a fruit farm to be able to survive these first few years.

As Mary wrote, this was no localized scourge, but an invasion that plagued Western farmers for over three years in the 1870s. Some readers may recall a similar account about grasshoppers in the stories of Laura Ingalls Wilder. In *On the Banks of Plum Creek,* Laura tells the story of the grasshoppers at her family's farm in Minnesota. They invaded in a massive swarm, ate all the Ingalls' wheat, laid their eggs, and then ominously marched west.[144] This fictionalized account describes what Laura Ingalls' family really did experience in Minnesota in the 1875-1876 years. As Wilder wrote in her autobiography, clouds of grasshoppers came, "their wings a shiny white making a screen between us and the sun. They were dropping to the ground like hail in a hailstorm faster and faster."[145] Despite the Ingalls

---

[142] Elsie Chambers does not even mention the grasshoppers in the years that the Chambers owned the ranch, only writing that, in the 1860s, "the flourishing crops of grain and garden produce were evidently too great a temptation to the grasshoppers to leave unmolested." Elsie Chambers, "What Happened While the Cabin Lived," 1.

[143] Mary Chambers DeLong, "The Chambers Family History," 3.

[144] Laura Ingalls Wilder, *On the Banks of Plum Creek* (New York: HarperCollins Publishers, 1971), 194.

[145] Laura Ingalls Wilder, *Pioneer Girl: The Annotated Autobiography* (Pierre, South Dakota: South Dakota Historical Society Press, 2014), 79.

family's best attempts, their crops were destroyed and their livelihood ruined. The blight continued past that year. This devastating infestation of the Rocky Mountain Locusts lasted from 1874 until 1877, consuming half of the country's agricultural production.[146] Western farmers had experienced grasshopper plagues before. None were as disastrous as this one. Farmers in Colorado, Kansas, Nebraska, Iowa, Minnesota, and the Dakota Territory were in such dire straits that the federal government began to take steps to intervene and provide aid.[147] This was the farming landscape into which the Chambers bought—a country plagued with grasshoppers, as seen in the Figure 20 map on page 69.

---

[146] Caroline, Fraser, ed, *Laura Ingalls Wilder: The Little House Books,* (New York: HarperCollins Publishers, Inc., 2012), 807.

[147] Fraser, 807. Army posts on the frontier supplied aid to some hurting farmers, and then the federal government formed an Entomological Commission of three prominent entomologists in order to assess the problem and come up with possible solutions. By the time they had gathered and published all their data, the years of locusts were over and there was nothing for the government to do. Theodore L. Hopkins, Extinction of the Rocky Mountain Locust, BioScience, Volume 55, Issue 1, January 2005, 80–81.

69

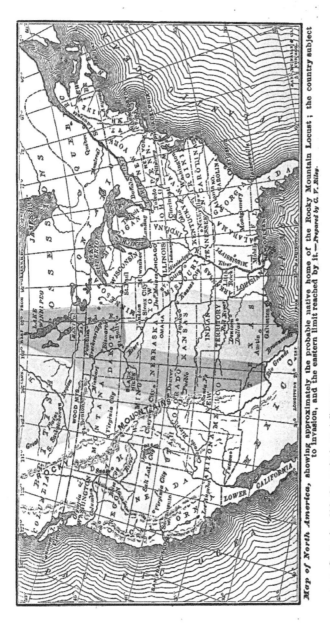

Map of North America, showing approximately the probable native home of the Rocky Mountain Locust; the country subject to invasion, and the eastern limit reached by it. —*Prepared by C. V. Riley.*

Country in which the species is not indigenous; which it visits at irregular intervals; in which it is most disastrous; and which it vacates within a year.

Region where the species comes to perfection; in which it permanently breeds; and from which come the disastrous swarms that sweep over the first mentioned region.

Area more often visited; in which the species holds its own longer, but which it generally forsakes in the course of time.

Area west of the mountains where the species also, in all probability, breeds permanently; from which it sometimes pushes to the east of the mountain range; and from which the California swarms probably come.

Figure 20 - Entomologist Charles Riley compiled this map of the reaches of the Rocky Mountain Locust in 1877.

70

Did the Chambers know the risks when they bought their property? Colorado pioneers had experienced Rocky Mountain locusts in smaller batches a few times in the 1860s, but never on this scale or for this many years. The first wave of grasshoppers invaded El Paso County shortly after the Chambers arrived in late spring 1874. *The Colorado Mountaineer,* a Colorado Springs newspaper, records that the locusts descended from the north on July 22, 1874—less than three weeks after the Chambers' daughter Bessie was born and months before they bought Rock Ledge Ranch.[148] In unprecedented and terrifying numbers the grasshoppers wreaked havoc as they never had before. Newspapers in fall 1874 lamented "the present devastation wrought by grasshoppers" and urged the careful stewarding of whatever resources remained.[149] Yet there would be no rest for the weary. Spring rolled around, and the eggs the grasshoppers had laid in the soil hatched on April 10th, 1875.[150] Still reeling from the destruction of 1874, farmers were once again thrust into an all-out war against the flying insects.

Firsthand accounts that remain communicate that these locusts were more than just a pest—they were a terror. In 1874, 1875, and 1876, swarms of grasshoppers arrived every summer "darkening the sun" like a "vast cloud" and proceeded to ravage everything they could get their jaws on.[151] Once they devoured everything in sight, they would lay their eggs in the ground and depart to ruin the next town (see illustration of this in Figure 21 on page 71). The eggs would hatch in late spring the following year, eat their fill, and then march or fly away *en masse*. Descriptions of these grasshopper clouds sound like a horrifying nightmare. Contemporary entomologist Charles Riley wrote that

> the noise of their jaw, when feeding, can be imagined by one who has
> fought a prairie fire, and has heard the peculiar cracking and grinding

---

148 *The Colorado Mountaineer,* February 21, 1877.

149 *Colorado Springs Gazette,* September 12, 1874.

150 *The Colorado Mountaineer,* February 21, 1877.

151 Grace DeLong, "A Ranch Begins," 3.

noise. When hard pushed for food, they will eat anything. They have been seen at work devouring the wool on the back of a sheep, and if one of their number is injured he is made to satisfy the hunger of some of his brethren. Carrion does not escape them, and dead animals are sometimes pounced upon and eaten.[152]

Professor Riley, who was hired by the federal government to investigate the problem, travelled throughout the West during these years to speak with farmers concerning the grasshoppers. He listened to their stories, heard their queries, and offered what knowledge and advice he had. The *Colorado Springs Gazette* dutifully announced his coming every time he visited to investigate or speak on "the grasshopper question," as the locals called it. He wrote a multitude of essays and articles about the habits of the Rocky Mountain locusts and potential solutions to their scourging of the West. Eventually, he successfully predicted the end of the plague—but he was unable to keep the pests from destroying thousands of farmers' crops in the meantime.

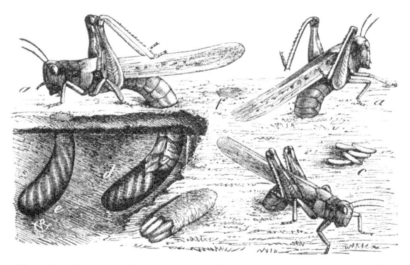

Figure 21 - Grasshopper laying eggs in the soil. Drawing from article by Professor Charles Riley, Entomologist, 1877.

---

[152] Charles Riley, in the *Colorado Springs Gazette,* June 12, 1875.

Colorado Springs newspapers in the 1874-1877 years were chock-full of locust announcements and anecdotes. "The grasshopper question" was a persistent problem which everyone was constantly trying to inform, solve, or make jokes about. The *Gazette* must have received some comments from readers about the immense amount of grasshopper coverage, for an editorial titled "THE GREAT ENEMY" in February 1877 declared that "The Gazette does not think it necessary to apologize for the amount of space it devotes to the grasshopper question."[153] Anticipating the next invasion in early 1875, farmers begged neighboring towns to inform them when the grasshoppers arrived and departed so that they could at least be aware of their advent, though there was often little to nothing they could do to mitigate the damage. On August 21st, the *Gazette* noted that the hoppers had returned and made some rather sarcastic comments about less than scathing treatments of grasshoppers in literature. Another story lamented "Is there a Pharaoh among us? Else why this plague?"[154]

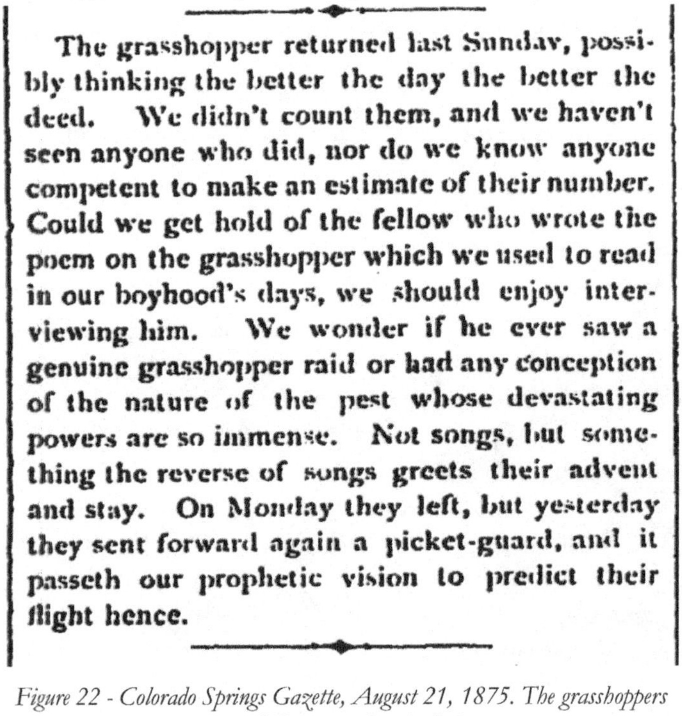

> The grasshopper returned last Sunday, possibly thinking the better the day the better the deed. We didn't count them, and we haven't seen anyone who did, nor do we know anyone competent to make an estimate of their number. Could we get hold of the fellow who wrote the poem on the grasshopper which we used to read in our boyhood's days, we should enjoy interviewing him. We wonder if he ever saw a genuine grasshopper raid or had any conception of the nature of the pest whose devastating powers are so immense. Not songs, but something the reverse of songs greets their advent and stay. On Monday they left, but yesterday they sent forward again a picket-guard, and it passeth our prophetic vision to predict their flight hence.

Figure 22 - Colorado Springs Gazette, August 21, 1875. The grasshoppers returned, far worse than in fiction.

---

[153] *Colorado Springs Gazette*, February 17, 1877.

[154] *Colorado Springs Gazette*, May 1, 1875.

Some suggested eating the grasshoppers, others burning them, others trapping them in a giant net raised by balloons.[155] The sheer number of times grasshoppers were mentioned in the news in the 1874-1877 years is enough to attest to the fact that the plague was an extremely influential event, culturally as well as agriculturally. One writer observed with fierce optimism that the citizens of Colorado Springs emerged more united because they had fought the grasshoppers together.[156] The papers in those days, like the wheat fields, were riddled with hoppers as the people struggled to survive in these early days of the settlement.

Yet between the humor and a determinedly positive outlook, the newspaper accounts tend to sound cheerful despite the devastation wrought by the grasshoppers. Certainly, the boosters in the city were attempting to downplay the disaster, concerned that the language of plague would slow or cease the settlement of the West. As for the citizens who contributed to the paper, they were trying to put a good face on a terrifying and devastating agricultural disaster. After the first invasion in 1874, one optimistic soul noted in early 1875 that Colorado was doing relatively well because, unlike Kansas, it was not entirely dependent on its crops to stay afloat.[157] In early 1876, the editors noted that despite more grasshopper attacks, "the year just past has not been a bad one for us, here in Colorado Springs. In the county of El Paso at large, of course our farmers are out of pocket on grasshopper account, but as most of them also own stock, they are not so very badly off after all."[158] (See the whole entry in Figure 23 on page 74.) This descibes

---

[155] *Colorado Springs Gazette,* February 17th, 1877. This was suggested by a man entering a competition in the state of Minnesota. The state government announced that they would award $600 cash (almost $15,000 in 2020 dollars) to someone who could come up with a solution to the grasshopper problem. Speaking of balloons, the *Gazette* also records an account from a man who was up in a balloon when a swarm of grasshoppers came by. He was horrified as the grasshoppers ate through his balloon, but he lived to tell the tale, for the army of grasshoppers flapped their wings and gently set down the balloon so the balloonist returned to earth unharmed. "We don't intend to vouch for the absolute truth of this anecdote," stated the *Gazette,* "but we got it from the balloonist himself, and he surely ought to know." *Colorado Springs Gazette,* October 9, 1875.

[156] *Colorado Springs Gazette,* August 14, 1875.

[157] *Colorado Springs Gazette,* January 30, 1875.

[158] *Colorado Springs Gazette,* January 22, 1876.

74

> Taken altogether, the year just past has not been a bad one for us, here in Colorado Springs.
>
> In the county of El Paso at large, of course our farmers are out of pocket on grasshopper account, but as most of them also own stock, they are not so very badly off after all. The year has been a splendid one for our stock interests, the grass on the range has been good, and still continues so, and stock has been and still is in fine order. In addition to this, our stockmen have been enabled to sell off their surplus stock at very remunerative figures.
>
> The prospects for 1876 are good, in an agricultural light. It is not anticipated that the grasshoppers will be around again, and our farmers are arranging to put into cultivation a larger acreage than ever before.

Figure 23 - Colorado Springs Gazette, January 22, 1876. Note the optimism at the end about the grasshoppers not being expected again in 1876. Sadly, it was not to be.

the situation of the Chambers family, and the key to their survival and subsequent success. Since they had the means to purchase dairy cows and keep their stock fed through these challenging years, they were able to ride out the grasshopper plague.

Though it was not what they first intended for their farm in Colorado, the Chambers' dairy operation successfully sustained them through the grasshopper years. Though writings by the Chambers family do not mention the scale of the Chambers dairy operation, their tax records indicate they had anywhere from ten to twenty milking cows in the late 1870s.[159] An 1876 newspaper advertisement, published in *The Colorado Mountaineer,* adds a little more detail to the story (see Figure 24 on page 75). The ad, announcing "Pure Milk!" reveals that the Chambers delivered milk, "as cheap as the cheapest" but with guaranteed quality. This ad fits with family histories that recalled the Chambers' dairy operation as their solution to the grasshopper question. Previous researchers have been under the impression that their dairy herd was small, but the Chambers 1878 tax schedule reports that they owned thirty dairy cattle—twenty mature for milking and ten yearlings.[160] The 1879 tax records report thirty-eight cows of mixed stock (meaning their herd could have

[159] 1878 Tax Schedule, R.M Chambers.

[160] Ibid.

included Texas cattle). By 1880 the number decreased to only ten head of cattle, and after that the tax schedules never record more than one or two cows.[161]

PURE MILK!

Delivered Daily in

COLORADO SPRINGS

As cheap as the cheapest.

Guaranteed as to Quality and Condition.

Leave orders on SLATE in the Postoffice.

R. M. CHAMBERS.

Figure 24 - The Colorado Mountaineer, December 20, 1876. Rock Ledge Ranch milk advertisement.

Although the Chambers did not focus on raising cattle for beef in their years at Rock Ledge Ranch, developments in cattle ranching during these years are worth noting because of the nationwide transition from open ranching on the plains to the stationary ranch. In the late 1850s and early 1860s, settlers discovered, to their great surprise, that the plains once called the "Great American Desert" provided more than sufficient grazing pastures for their cows. Early Colorado immigrants describe setting their cows loose on the prairie unsure if they would survive the winter, only to find them sleek and fat from prairie grass come spring.[162] Boosters lost no time in declaring how perfect the Great Plains were for feeding cattle all year round. Charles Goodnight brought the first herd of Texas cows up to Colorado in 1866, and more soon followed. Cattlemen worked with the legislature to develop laws that allowed for privately owned and branded cattle to graze on unsettled public land on the plains. Every year the cows were herded together and

[161] Tax Schedules, R.M. Chambers, 1879, 1880, 1884, 1885.

[162] Abbott, Leonard, and Noel, *Colorado: A History of the Centennial State,* 170.

then split up according to the different ranchers' brands to be sold in the fall.[163] Cattle ranching was a booming business for both ranchers and investors by 1880. There were 800,000 cattle in the state of Colorado alone and the cows were selling for up to $40 a head—nearly $1,100 each in today's money.[164] These were the golden years of the cowboy.

As with most booms, however, it was swiftly followed by a bust. Blizzards and droughts from 1884-1887 meant many ranchers' prospects dropped dead as swiftly as their cows. Combined with hard years economically as the price of beef declined, and an 1885 law that forbade the fencing in of public lands, the cattle trade changed dramatically.[165] Ranchers had to abandon cattle ranching entirely or adopt new methods as the country transitioned to ranching that was based in privately owned lands with wells and fences.[166] The glory days of the cowboy were over. What about the Chambers cows? The Chambers tax records report that they owned some Texas or mixed breed cattle in 1879 and 1880, but their 1884 records only mention one dairy cow. It appears that the Chambers' foray into cattle at Rock Ledge Ranch did not last beyond the turn of the decade, and thus the dropping beef prices did not affect their farming prospects. The cows and the dairy had been an interim source of income, something to last them through the years of grasshopper plague. It served its purpose: diversification and the raising of stock saved them as the swarms of grasshoppers consumed all the green things they could find to eat.

Blessedly, the plague did come to an end. Though people were wary after three years of grasshopper infestation, they entered 1877 somewhat optimistic. Professor Riley predicted that the grasshoppers would not be returning, and he was

[163] Abbott, Leonard, and Noel, *Colorado: A History of the Centennial State,* 172.

[164]Ibid.

[165] Noel, Mahoney, and Stevens, *Historical Atlas of Colorado,* 19.

[166] Brands, 391.

correct.[167] Week after week through the spring, summer, and fall Colorado Springs newspapers timidly observed that the grasshoppers had not yet returned and perhaps they would not. This time, they were correct. Never again did the country see such a plague of grasshoppers as it did in these years. By the early 1900s, the Rocky Mountain locust was completely extinct. One writer notes in September of 1877 that the grasshoppers were gone, having driven out the easily discouraged farmers, leaving only those who were committed to hard work.[168] That certainly described the Chambers. When confronted with hardship, they diversified and found a way through. The cows are only one example of their ingenuity. Taking in boarders also provided income during these years. By 1877 they had expanded their boarding house to serve as a restaurant, too. Guests—perhaps working men, perhaps tourists visiting Garden of the Gods for the day—could stop in to the Rock Ledge House between noon and two p.m. and pay for a hearty, home-cooked meal.[169] The Chambers were innovative entrepreneurs, not afraid of hard work. Having survived the grasshopper plague, they now had another Colorado challenge to face: lack of water.

The clouds of grasshoppers may have been too many, but the clouds of rain were far too few in the West. Early explorers, notably John Wesley Powell, had described how arid the region west of the 100th meridian was.[170] The western half of North America gets significantly less rain than the eastern half, so farmers could not depend on rainfall to water their crops (see the Figure 25 map on page 78). Colorado gets about seventeen inches of precipitation per year, on average.[171] In comparison, Pennsylvania rainfall averages around forty-two inches per year—so

---

[167] *Colorado Springs Gazette,* July 14, 1877.

[168] *Colorado Springs Gazette,* September 15, 1877.

[169] *Colorado Springs Gazette,* July 28, 1877. This advertisement is in Figure 26 on page 82.

[170] Brands, 411.

[171] Noel, Mahoney, and Stevens, *Historical Atlas of Colorado,* 19.

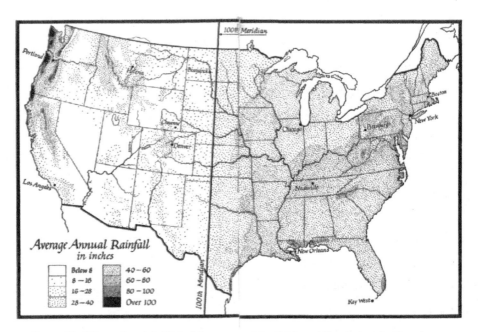

Figure 25 - The portion of the United States east of the 100th meridian receives significantly more rain than the western half. (Map from Great Plains Trail.)

pioneers such as the Chambers were used to more than twice as much rain. This scared the boosters who were eagerly promoting Colorado. Without farmers, the territory might boom but would inevitably bust, for it could not support its mines without food for the miners to eat.[172] The dryness that drew the consumptives to Colorado would drive away the farmers, if they could not learn how to water by irrigation. Irrigation was an unfamiliar technique to most Eastern farmers, and it was complicated. Farmers had to correctly calculate the exact timing, the proper quantity, and which crops to favor when watering by irrigation.[173] Those who managed it well, such as early settlers in the Greeley agricultural colony, claimed it was both safer and more productive than relying on rainfall because it was a more steady source of water.[174] Learning to irrigate properly, let alone changing the land and constructing the mechanisms to make it happen, was no small task.

---

[172] Abbott, Leonard, and Noel, *Colorado: A History of the Centennial State,* 163.

[173] Ibid.

[174] Noel, Mahoney, and Stevens, *Historical Atlas of Colorado,* 19.

Furthermore, farmers throughout the West quickly learned that building an irrigation system called for community and teamwork. Irrigation required long canals and ditches to deliver water, and in dry years the ditches were not always enough. Settlers would have to build reservoirs to store water from wet years for dry years.[175] This was not something that the independent homesteader could accomplish by himself. He needed to work with his neighbors, as the Chambers did. Although they had managed to secure a piece of land with good water on it by Colorado standards, Mary Chambers DeLong records that "the water didn't seem to be sufficient" for all the Chambers' agricultural endeavors.[176] To make their land as productive as they wished, they needed to ensure their water sources would be more abundant and consistent than Camp Creek and the springs on the property, all of which varied in water flow throughout the year. Mr. Chambers worked with two neighbors, Hardwick and Neff, who lived further south down the Camp Creek Valley, to dig ditches and build a reservoir in order to water their crops.[177]

Thankfully, some of this work had already been begun by earlier settlers. The three neighbors improved upon a ditch that brought water from Camp Creek into the 160 acres that the Chambers bought from Walter Galloway—a ditch that Galloway probably dug during his years on the property (Camp Creek Ditch No. 1).[178] They built a second surveyed ditch, parallel to the first one but farther west, that brought water from higher up the creek in Glen Eyrie (Neff, Hardwick, and Chambers Ditch No. 2).[179] Each ditch would have been at least a mile long and a few feet wide to handle the water that flowed down from the mountains during spring snowmelt and summer rainstorms. This water flowed on the back side of

[175] Abbott, Leonard, and Noel, *Colorado: A History of the Centennial State,* 166.

[176] Mary Chambers DeLong, "Chambers Family History," 3.

[177] Grace DeLong, "A Ranch Begins: The Chambers Period 1874-1900," 3.

[178] This ditch ran south from about the location of the Glen Eyrie gatehouse to the white barn that is now on the ranch. Smaller ditches were constructed running east into which the water could be released in order to water the crops.

[179] Mary Chambers DeLong, "Chambers Family History," 3.

the hogback ridge between the Rock Ledge House and the Garden of the Gods. Chambers and his neighbors built up the natural basin area behind the house into a reservoir, fed by the higher ditch.[180] This reservoir, probably four to five hundred feet in diameter, is visible in pictures of the ranch from this era, a shining white surface between the Rock Ledge House and the Garden of the Gods rocks.[181] To this day, the area that served as the reservoir is remarkably green and fertile compared to the surrounding area, and some pieces of the irrigation features like head gates remain on the hill side. Chambers, with three young children, a house full of boarders, and a dairy to run, never could have accomplished this on his own. Working with his neighbors, however, he was able to set up the whole Camp Creek Valley for success. The ditches and reservoir Chambers, Neff, and Hardwick built would provide enough water to make the Chambers' farm one of the most productive in the county. When it came to irrigation in Colorado, however, building the irrigation ditches was only half of the work; farmers also had a legal battle to fight.

Though it may seem a dry subject, water laws in Colorado have a fascinating history. When the Colorado Constitutional Convention met in 1875, they knew that men were already waging wars over water. The traditional water laws people were accustomed to from back East were as insufficient as the water they tried to apportion. Those laws stipulated that only those who owned land along the watercourse could use it, and they could not divert the water away from that watercourse. Irrigation, which was the only way to farm in Colorado, required diverting the flow of water. So the legislators struck out in a different direction, writing into the Colorado Constitution the Doctrine of Prior Appropriation.[182] This stated that "the right to divert the unappropriated waters of any natural

---

[180] Carol Kennis Lopez, "Agricultural Legacy: Rock Ledge Ranch Historic Site," 11, and Grace DeLong, "A Ranch Begins: The Chambers Period 1874-1900," 6. Grace DeLong writes that in the winter, the Chambers and their friends skated on the reservoir.

[181] See Figure 30, the picture labelled "Pikes Peak" on page 92.

[182] Abbott, Leonard, and Noel, *Colorado: A History of the Centennial State,* 168.

stream to beneficial uses shall never be denied. Priority of appropriation shall give the better right as between those using water for the same purpose."[183] The Constitution further stipulated that domestic purposes had priority above other purposes, and agricultural purposes had priority over manufacturing purposes. In other words, the law stated that water rights in Colorado were first come, first served. Whoever was there first could divert and use as much of the water as he wanted. Colorado water law was written with irrigation specifically in mind, and other western states modelled their water laws after it.[184]

This did not mean, however, that the battles about water were over. Legislation in 1879 and 1881 organized the state into different districts for water claims and appointed water commissioners to determine who had prior rights to a flow of water. These commissioners would settle disputes over water rights via suits and hearings in state courts. Robert Chambers, who with his neighbors "had first rights to the water of Camp Creek which ran through the ranch," did not assume that he would be able to maintain those rights without some work.[185] He apparently kept well-informed of developments in water law and took the necessary steps to ensure his legal ownership of the water he was using on his land. In 1879 he was able to register both ditches that he and his neighbors had built and claim prior appropriation through written evidence that the ditches on his and his neighbors' properties had prior claim on the water.[186]

Characteristically, the Chambers did not waste time when there was something to be done. They continued to guard their water rights carefully throughout their years in Colorado. In 1888, the Hardwicks complained that William Watson, who

---

[183] Article XVI, Sections 5 and 6, Constitution of the State of Colorado, 1876, in Abbott, Leonard, and Noel, 169.

[184] Abbott, Leonard, and Noel, 169.

[185] Mary Chambers DeLong, "Chambers Family History," 3.

[186] Carol Kennis Lopez, "Agricultural Legacy: Rock Ledge Ranch Historic Site," 10. Lopez notes that the ditches are registered as being claimed in 1864 and 1874, respectively—so at least one of them must have been built by Galloway or perhaps even a prior settler to him.

apparently lived nearby in the Camp Creek Valley, was "maliciously" damaging the Neff, Hardwick, and Chambers ditch. The three men filed an injunction against Watson, and the November 17, 1888 *Gazette* reported that they successfully defended their water—and therefore their livelihood—from harm.[187] The doctrine of prior appropriation and the legal work of Robert Chambers meant that the Camp Creek water rights stayed safely with the ranch property through the Chambers years.

Even before their water was secured or defended, however, the Chambers were putting it to use growing fruits and vegetables. By no means did they waste the grasshopper years. They spent them developing other ways to grow and protect their crops. An advertisement placed in the Colorado Springs Gazette in July 1877 provides evidence of another way the Chambers were generating income (see Figure 26 below).

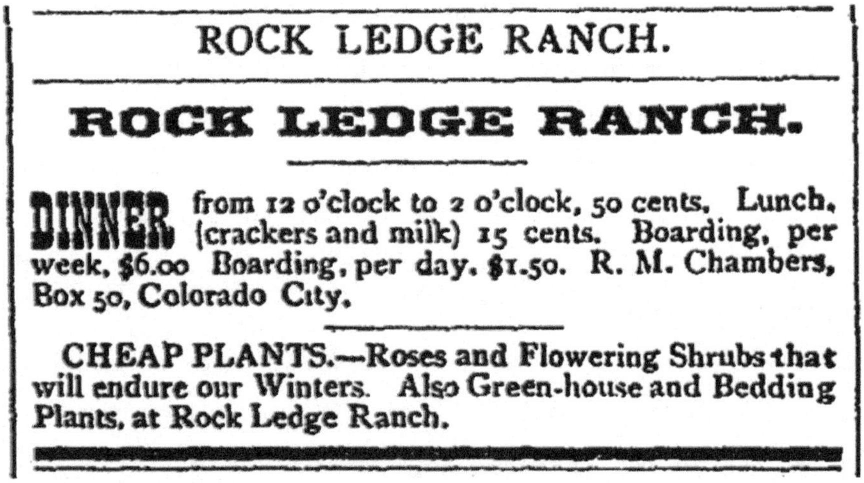

ROCK LEDGE RANCH.

ROCK LEDGE RANCH.

DINNER from 12 o'clock to 2 o'clock, 50 cents. Lunch, (crackers and milk) 15 cents. Boarding, per week, $6.00 Boarding, per day, $1.50. R. M. Chambers, Box 50, Colorado City.

CHEAP PLANTS.—Roses and Flowering Shrubs that will endure our Winters. Also Green-house and Bedding Plants, at Rock Ledge Ranch.

Figure 26 - Rock Ledge Ranch "Dinner" ad. Placed in Colorado Springs Gazette July through September, 1877.

Under the all-caps proclamation of "DINNER" under "ROCK LEDGE RANCH," the ad reveals that in addition to taking in boarders and serving lunches, the Chambers were selling "Green-house Plants." The sale of plants was likely a

---

[187] Lopez., 11.

very lucrative business in the first summer after the end of the grasshopper plague. But what does the ad mean by "Green-house Plants?"

Mary Chambers DeLong and other descendants and sources record that Robert Chambers designed and built two steam-heated greenhouses, which appear to have been about twenty feet by thirty feet.[188] Located just behind the Rock Ledge House, the glass panels of its roof can be seen, stark white compared to the rocky surroundings, in a circa 1880 photograph of the house and family. Pieces of broken

Figure 27 - The glass panels that formed the roofs of the greenhouses can be seen behind the house to the left in this picture Courtesy Bruce W. Dunbar Family Collection.

glass from this greenhouse continue to wash up from the ground behind the house whenever it rains. Because the greenhouses were heated by steam, the Chambers could grow fruits, vegetables, flowers, and other plants year-round. So even in the winter, the Chambers could supply the nearby Antlers Hotel with fresh fruits and vegetables grown in their greenhouses.[189] They also sold their produce in the form of jams, jellies, and preserves that Mrs. Chambers made.[190] Between a relatively steady source of water and their greenhouses, the Chambers could weather many

---

[188] Grace DeLong, "A Ranch Begins: The Chambers Period 1874-1900," 4. Some descendants note that Ben Chambers also played a role in the construction of these greenhouses, but as he would have been only eight years old at the time, it may be that this refers to later maintenance and improvements on the greenhouses, not the original design and building of them. He certainly learned much from being involved in the family's agricultural technology, however, because he became a plumber as an adult. Grace also records that the greenhouses kept the little girls busy "puttying the hundreds of glass panes in the green houses."

[189] Loe, *Life in the Altitudes,* 53.

[190] Grace DeLong, "A Ranch Begins: The Chambers Period 1874-1900," 4.

84

agricultural storms. The timing of the ad placed in the *Gazette* reveals that the Chambers conceived of the idea for the greenhouse and likely put it into use reasonably early in their time at the ranch. If by July 1877 they were selling plants grown in it, it must have been constructed, at the latest, that spring.

Greenhouses were not uncommon in Colorado Springs in these years. The Chambers would have had several competitors in their greenhouse plants business. As early as 1873, the *Colorado Springs Gazette* announced that one of the categories for agriculture competitions at the fair was "best variety of greenhouse plants."[191] Ostensibly enough people were using greenhouses that they earned their own competitive category. In 1875, William L.G. Soule posted several advertisements for plants and trees from his Experimental Greenhouse Garden, "near the depot" in Colorado Springs. One ad is for evergreens, while another announces that he has "Greenhouse and

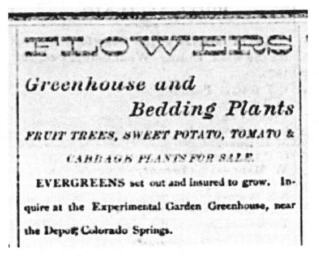

Figure 28 - Colorado Mountaineer, Oct 21, 1875. Mr. Soule was apparently conducting a business similar to the one the Chambers eventually ran.

Bedding Plants, fruit trees, sweet potato, tomato, and cabbage plants for sale."[192] As this ad was run two years before the Chambers' notice of a similar nature, it is even possible that the Chambers bought their saplings and plants from Mr. Soule to get started, though this is speculation. At the very least, however, they ran very similar businesses from their greenhouses—both advertise "Greenhouse and Bedding Plants." The term used in this time period for this kind of business is

---

[191] *Colorado Springs Gazette,* February 22, 1873.

[192] *The Colorado Mountaineer,* October 21, 1875.

"Market Garden"—growing plants for sale. The multitude of sunny days in Colorado meant that if one could only keep plants warm and watered in a greenhouse, the growing season could last all year long. The Chambers, wasting nothing, made good use of this.

These Experimental Garden Greenhouse ads also shed light on the kind of plants the Chambers would have bought and sold. Mr. Soule was selling and setting out evergreen saplings—a great need in Colorado Springs, a city initially devoid of trees. People planning to stick around for years to come wanted to plant trees that would eventually provide wind breaks for their homes (and sometimes for their gardens and orchards as well), so selling trees and other plants was a profitable business. It was saplings, not seeds, that were the important commodity—once the farmers figured out what they could grow, of course. Thankfully, the Chambers were not on their own in this regard. They were not the earliest pioneer fruit growers in Colorado—by the time they could finally grow fruit after the locusts ceased to plague them, some farmers had already compiled wisdom and experience they could share about what worked and what did not in the Colorado climate.

As they were wont to do with other aspects of the West, boosters made Colorado sound like the Promised Land for fruit growing. Perhaps this is another reason the Chambers chose to start a fruit farm. In 1872, the *Out West* declared that "fruit growing in Colorado is an accomplished fact" and that "every owner of land…should plant fruit trees."[193] Today, Colorado does produce quality fruit—but most fruit farms are on the west side of the Rocky Mountains, where the water is more plentiful, or further south and east than Colorado Springs. Not so in the 1870s and 1880s, as settlements near Denver and Colorado Springs filled with farmers eager to grow fruit. The late 1860s through the early 1880s were years of experimental farming in Colorado—and in many places, including the Chambers ranch, it proved very rewarding. Just as with water, the community element of farming was crucial with fruit growing. As the Colorado Springs Colony got

[193] *Out West*, July 18, 1872, and November 21, 1872.

started, they looked north to the agricultural colony of Greeley to see what they had grown successfully. Newspapers were an important means of communication between towns throughout Colorado, as they were for grasshopper news. The *Out West* in the early 1870s regularly quoted lines from Greeley and Denver papers that named farmers whose efforts were bearing fruit. By 1883, a society of farmers and fruitgrowers who had been meeting regularly to compare notes and present papers on their fruit-growing efforts published a short work entitled *Fruit Culture in Colorado*. The book was mostly a compilation of advice from fruit growers across the state. It contained guidance on apples, cherries, pears, peaches, plums, blackberries, raspberries, currants, goosberries, strawberries, and grapes—all of which could be grown successfully in Colorado at the time, they concluded, except peaches.[194] Major Henry McAllister, one of the founders of Colorado Springs, was quoted several times in the chapter on apples. His experimental garden and orchard at his home in Colorado Springs produced both a multitude of apples and much agricultural wisdom, which he generously shared.[195] Though the farmers often disagreed on windbreaks, fertilizer, and how best to battle pests, they presented their findings in this book in order to aid others interested in horticulture.

After fifteen years of experimentation, farmers were quick to acknowledge that fruit growing was not as easy as pie. For example, with apples and most other fruits, horticulturalists discovered that precise irrigation work was required. Farmers lost entire orchards because of too much or too little water.[196] Beyond the ever-present problem of water, fruit growers in Colorado faced many other challenges. Colorado's late snows and frosts meant that farmers needed hardy trees

---

[194] William Edgar Pabor, *Fruit Culture in Colorado: A Manual of Information* (Denver: W.E. Pabor, Publisher, 1883).

[195] Eric Metzger, the Executive Director of the McAllister House Museum in Colorado Springs, has completed extensive research on McAllister's contributions to Colorado agriculture, and was instrumental in helping me understand the agricultural landscape in Colorado at this time, through both conversations and resources that pointed me in the right direction.

[196] Pabor, 15.

whose blossoms could survive late frosts, or they would lose fruit crops year after year.[197] The fierce Front Range winds also proved an obstacle for many reasons. McAllister and his peers debated over the efficacy of wind breaks for their orchards—some declared fruit trees could not succeed without them, while others argued that the wind-hardened trees at the borders were the most fruitful in their orchards.[198] The Chambers were certainly aware of the dangers of wind—Robert and Ben Chambers at one point built a windmill to help with the movement of water on the ranch, but it was "ruined by the first big wind."[199] Harsh winters and bugs posed other problems that were best solved by finding varieties of trees and bushes that resisted them best. If all this was not enough, hail could cause an otherwise perfect crop to be lost in a matter of minutes.[200] This little book compiled by the agricultural society represented many years of trial and error experimentation. It would have been an invaluable tool in the hands of a Colorado fruit farmer.

Though these farmers and horticulturalists often disagreed on certain methods, by the time their book was published in 1883 they also had significant advice to give as to what worked. Henry McAllister, having written to a New England apple grower and tested out his advice, had found varieties of apples that robustly resisted the late frosts.[201] Others had discovered that although sweet cherries often struggled, tart or sour cherries did far better in the Colorado climate.[202] They also

---

[197] Pabor., 18.

[198] Ibid., 16.

[199] Mary Chambers DeLong, "Chambers Family History," 3. Today a period-accurate windmill exists on the ranch, though it is obviously not the one the Chambers built. It is also not in the same position as the Chambers' would have been. Mary Chambers DeLong describes the position of this short-lived windmill as "north of the reservoir," which would put it behind the hog-back ridge that runs behind the Rock Ledge House.

[200] Pabor, 52.

[201] Ibid., 18.

[202] Pabor, 30-32. Today, in order to restore Rock Ledge Ranch to a similar state as it was during the Chambers years, Rock Ledge Ranch has a small orchard of cherry trees—a small, tart pie cherry that has been successfully resisting late frosts. Rock Ledge Ranch Historic Site seeks to replicate what

praised the cherry as a Colorado fruit because cherry trees did not require as much water as other fruit trees. Some farmers recommended dwarf varieties of fruit trees as more hardy and resistant to heat, cold, pests, and drought.[203] Overall, the amount of work that went into this little Colorado fruit growers handbook is tremendous, and it was a lifesaver for many farmers.

Were Robert and Elsie Chambers aware of this work? Seeing as it was not yet in existence when they first planted their orchards and other fruit bushes and plants, they would not have had access to this resource when they began growing fruit. They would have had to discover these practices through trying their own experimentation, talking with other horticulturalists, or scouring the newspapers. Yet the fruits they succeeded with match those of their contemporaries. In fact, they grew the greater part of the list of fruits covered in *Fruit Culture in Colorado*— apples, cherries, strawberries, raspberries, gooseberries, and currants. In her account "What Happened While the Cabin Lived," Mrs. Chambers lists their produce as "six acres of asparagus, hundreds of apple trees and hundreds of cherry trees besides other fruit."[204] The asparagus apparently kept coming up for years after the Chambers were gone. At least one remnant of the orchard has lasted even longer. One apple tree that the Chambers planted still stands at Rock Ledge Ranch. Affectionately called "Old Rosie," the tree still bears fruit most years despite a huge hole through her trunk and late frosts that attempt to thwart her. She is the last remaining representative of an impressive fruit enterprise. Tax records and agricultural census reports verify that the Chambers had one acre of fruit orchard

---

the Chambers did in other ways, too. On the 1878 tax records, two swine are listed, and so the ranch procures two piglets each spring and raises them into nice fat hogs all summer and fall, to be butchered in November. The Chambers' tax records also list horses, harnesses, and carriages, and today four horses call the ranch home. Furthermore, Rock Ledge Ranch is in the process of fundraising and planning for the construction of a greenhouse that will be a replica of what the Chambers built.

[203] Ibid., 21.

[204] Elsie Chambers, "What Happened While the Cabin Lived," 6.

in 1884 and three acres in 1885.[205] The beginnings of the orchard are visible in the foreground of the next picture, Figure 29, taken in approximately 1881.

Figure 29 - Eleanor and Mary Chambers in the Chambers' apple orchard, 1881. Courtesy Bruce W. Dunbar Family Collection.

The two girls in the field are Eleanor and Mary Chambers, who would have been about eight and six years old, respectively, when this picture was taken. The Rock Ledge House is visible on the right, and trees that are likely the start of the Chambers' orchards can be seen behind the girls. One can also pick out the long, glass roof of the greenhouse behind the house. They also had fifteen acres of "native grasses" that were presumably used for hay, because Robert Chambers lists a mowing machine and a hay rake on his 1879 taxes.[206]

What of the "other fruit?" The tax records specify that the Chambers had three acres of small fruit.[207] "Small fruit" or the "other fruit" Mrs. Chambers mentioned

---

[205] Tax Schedules, R.M. Chambers, 1884 and 1885.

[206] Tax Schedules, R.M. Chambers, 1879 and 1884.

[207] Tax Schedules, R.M. Chambers, 1884 and 1885.

included currants, gooseberries, strawberries, and raspberries.[208] Newspapers at the time show that these are fairly common fruits—listings of farms for sale at this time noted the raspberries, strawberries, gooseberries, and currants grown there.[209] Thus it appears that the Chambers' production is fairly typical of what Colorado fruit growers produced in those years—although Elsie W. Chambers maintained that the ranch had "grown more fruits and vegetables than any other ranch in El Paso County."[210] Other sources seem to confirm that even if this superlative was not exactly the case, Rock Ledge Ranch certainly had a good name in fruit. It is well-established that the Chambers supplied the prestigious Antlers Hotel with fruits and vegetables all year round. As the Antlers was a luxurious establishment with seventy-five guest rooms and suites, the Chambers' agricultural operation was clearly successful in terms of quality and quantity of fruit.[211]

To accomplish all this, the Chambers certainly needed help, and records indicate that they had it. Their census records from 1880 and 1885 include non-family members who apparently resided and worked at the ranch. In 1880, three men—Jacob Steiner, John Krug, and Frank Murr, all in their early twenties—are listed without any explanation about their connection to the family.[212] It is likely that they were farmhands assisting the Chambers around the ranch. Similarly, in the 1885 Colorado census two unrelated men, probably farmhands, are listed under Robert Chambers. This time the two men (William Roder and William Clark) are

---

[208] Tax Schedules, R.M. Chambers, 1884 and 1885.

[209] *Colorado Springs Gazette,* June 16, 1875, and *Queen Bee,* October 3, 1888.

[210] Elsie Chambers, "What Happened While the Cabin Lived," 6.

[211] Loe, *Life in the Altitudes,* 53.

[212] "United States Census, 1880," database with images, *FamilySearch* (https://familysearch.org/ark:/61903/1:1:MFDF-535: 19 February 2021), R M Chambers, Township 13 South Range 67 West, El Paso, Colorado, United States; citing enumeration district ED 45, sheet 469A, NARA microfilm publication T9 (Washington, D.C.: National Archives and Records Administration, n.d.), FHL microfilm 1,254,090. Also interesting to note: all three of these men are listed as from Ohio. Robert Chambers is listed in these census records as a "gardner" [sic].

listed with the role of "servant."[213] It is reasonable to assume these were farmhands employed by the Chambers, because Elsie Chambers mentions in passing that the ranch had employees, saying that "the employees of the ranch also made the cabin their rendezvous when the day's work was done" in her account of the ranch's history.[214] Two different young women are also mentioned in these censuses: a Mary Horton, age twenty-three, in 1880, and a Mari Conklin, age forty, in 1885.[215] Little to nothing is known about these women. Since they are listed under Robert Chambers on the census it is assumed that they lived on the ranch, possibly in one of the smaller upstairs bedrooms of the house. Between everything that needed to be accomplished with the farm work, the boarders, raising children, and cooking and preserving food, it is unsurprising that Mrs. Chambers would have had help around the house.

The physical evidence around the Rock Ledge House today suggests that the Chambers were prepared to store the produce they were growing. To this day, a root cellar remains, dug into the hill behind the kitchen of the Rock Ledge House. In the sandy soil where the house is built, a cellar underneath the house was not possible. Pictures taken after the turn of the century, however, indicate that what now stands is only part of what once existed. The photos show that at one point, the root cellar extended all the way from the hillside to the back of the kitchen, which is about ten yards, and could be entered directly from the kitchen. A root cellar would have been essential for keeping milk cold, storing the vegetables and fruit preserves they were growing and producing, and of course keeping their own foods and ingredients cool and dry. The part of the root cellar that remains to this day would have been the "wet" part of the root cellar, storing the foods that needed to be kept colder like butter and milk. Dug into the hill as it is, this part of

---

[213] "Colorado State Census, 1885," database with images, *FamilySearch* (https://familysearch.org/ark:/61903/1:1:K8WF-WP7: 4 March 2021), Robt Chamber, 1885; citing NARA microfilm publication M158 (Washington, D.C.: National Archives and Records Administration, n.d.); FHL microfilm 498, 506.

[214] Elsie Chambers, "What Happened While the Cabin Lived," 5.

[215] United States Census, 1880 and Colorado State Census, 1885.

the cellar remains remarkably cool even on the hottest summer days. The part that no longer stands would have been the "dry" part, for storing all the foods that need to be kept in the dark and dry but not necessarily cold.

Figure 30 - Photo of Rock Ledge Ranch from opposing ridge, date unknown. Courtesy Bruce W. Dunbar family collection.

Old photos, such as in Figure 30, show other small structures and outbuildings on the ranch property, about which little to nothing is known. The cabin that Walter Galloway constructed served as a shelter for the Chambers' livestock for several years before the Chambers eventually tore it down.[216] Tax records indicate that the Chambers always had a few horses and sometimes a couple of pigs, which

---

[216] Elsie's gift with words shines through as she tells this part of the story: "The cabin has been torn down and the four-footed travelers brought to mind Will Carleton's poem, 'Out of the Old House into the New," by forgetting their new stable and standing in their wonted place, behind a few posts and under a few boards that were left, and calling for their feed, wondering where their table had gone. And when nothing but the stone chimney was left, Dot and Dora stood face to face close to the old chimney condoling [sic] each other for the loss of the old home." Elsie Chambers, "What Happened While the Cabin Lived," 6.

would have needed shelter.[217] Also visible in this picture is the reservoir to the west of the house and the Chambers' fenced-in fields to the east, north, and south of it.

The Chambers continued their farming enterprises until they sold Rock Ledge Ranch in 1900. During Eleanor and Mary's high school years, writes Grace DeLong, "the family would spend the winters in town" and the summers back on the ranch.[218] This would have been in the late 1880s and into the 1890s. By this point, "the ranch had become a prosperous operation," states Grace, and it "must have been left to hired help during the school months."[219]

In 1900, when Robert and Elsie "wanted to retire from Colorado farming," they sold Rock Ledge Ranch to their neighbor, General William Jackson Palmer (see Figure 31 for the Gazette's announcement of Palmer's purchase).[220]

General William J. Palmer has purchased the Chambers ranch of about 160 acres for $17,000. It is located south of Glen Eyrie and is one of the most valuable in the country. With the ranch General Palmer has 1,500 acres in one body.

Figure 31 - Colorado Springs Gazette, April 7, 1900.

What motivated this sale? In October 1898, the Antlers Hotel burned to the ground. Though it was rebuilt, the project was not completed until 1901. The

---

[217] Tax Schedules, R.M. Chambers, 1878, 1879, 1884, and 1885.

[218] Grace DeLong, "A Ranch Begins: The Chambers Period 1874-1900," 6. She sweetly adds "but when summer came, they all returned to the place they loved best." One of their addresses in town was 529 E. Willamette Ave, but because several addresses are listed through the years, it is believed that they moved around in the city.

[219] Grace DeLong, "A Ranch Begins: The Chambers Period 1874-1900," 6.

[220] Mary Chambers DeLong, *Chambers Family History,* 4. In 1900, Robert Chambers was 62 and Elsie was 55. One wonders if the economic difficulties of the 1890s played any part in their retirement from farming in 1900. Another event that may have resulted in difficulty for them was that the Antlers Hotel burned down in 1898. That was a major source of income for the Chambers, so it is possible and even likely that this tragedy played a role in their decision to retire. They were clearly not in completely dire straits, however, for they spent a few years vacationing before settling down in Pasadena, California.

Antlers had been the Chambers' largest customer, so its destruction was a factor in the Chambers' decision to sell. As the *Gazette* and the Chambers' descendants record, Palmer paid the Chambers $17,000 for Rock Ledge Ranch—the equivalent of $540,000 in today's money. One of the greatest attractions of the land for Palmer was the water rights that came with the property. Because Chambers and his neighbors, Hardwick and Neff, had priority on the water due to the Colorado water law doctrine of prior appropriation, only by acquiring the land that had the first claim could Palmer obtain ownership of all the water that flowed down Queen's Canyon and through Glen Eyrie.[221]

With the money from the sale of the ranch, Robert and Elsie Chambers and their daughter Mary spent a few years travelling the country before settling down in Pasadena, California, in December 1903. Grace Delong implies that perhaps they had intended to attempt another fruit farm, but they discovered that "raising oranges in California was more than 'just lying under a tree and picking the fruit.'"[222] So in the end their move to California resulted in a true retirement from farming.

Strictly looking at their productive output, one can easily conclude that the Chambers succeeded agriculturally at Rock Ledge Ranch. They increased the value of their property twelve-fold in the twenty-five years they farmed there. The value of the legacy they leave behind is even greater to us today. The stories, photos, records, and trees that remain—not to mention the house itself!—paint for us a picture of farming in Colorado Springs in the last quarter of the nineteenth century. They faced wind, drought, cold, and grasshoppers, yet succeeded with cows, orchards, greenhouses, and more. Their struggles reveal the determination that the Colorado frontier required of farmers, and their victories display the

---

[221] It is clear that Palmer mostly wanted the property for the water rights. In 1907 Palmer built a large home in the Cape Town Colonial Dutch Style on the Rock Ledge Ranch property, a house called the "Orchard House" because of the orchards left by the Chambers. This house was briefly inhabited by Palmer's half-sister-in-law and her husband, Charlotte and William Sclater. The Orchard House still stands at Rock Ledge Ranch as well.

[222] Grace DeLong, "A Ranch Begins: The Chambers Period 1874-1900," 7.

ingenuity that it brought out of those as hardworking and dedicated as the Chambers. Elsie Chambers described Rock Ledge Ranch's agricultural legacy best when she wrote "its value has increased many fold and shown what even the apparent barren land, so near the foothills, may become by patient persistent effort."[223] For that is the best way to describe the story the Chambers leave: patient persistent effort.

---

[223] Elsie Chambers, "What Happened While the Cabin Lived," 6.

Chapter Four

"Strive Hard…in Good Faith"
The Chambers as Citizens of Colorado Springs, the Anti-Frontier Town

Robert Chambers' siblings had been concerned about the "tough going of the new life in that terrible far west [sic]," but the Colorado Springs that the Chambers inhabited was fighting with all its might to throw off the stereotype of the rugged frontier.[224] The Colorado Springs Company's vision of a perfect little community at the base of the Rockies intended to exclude the violence, immorality, and instability that plagued many western towns. How could one create such an anti-frontier town? Furthermore, how could one keep it? Churches, schools, and religious organizations were essential in both attracting the right kinds of people and maintaining a "generic Christian morality" once they arrived.[225] During their years at Rock Ledge Ranch between 1874 and 1900, the Chambers family illustrates the centrality of all three kinds of institutions. The Chambers were upright, industrious, and temperate people, constantly working to preserve Christian morality and better their community. Their faithful involvement in church, school, and ecumenical organizations not only demonstrates how they fit into their place in history but also reflects the story of the development of Colorado Springs.

---

[224] Mary Chambers DeLong, "The Chambers Family History," 3.

[225] Gregory Atkins, "'Business Sense If Not Souls': Boosters and Religion in Colorado Springs, 1871-1909" (*The Journal of the Gilded Age and Progressive Era* 17, no. 1, 2018), 78. Atkins' article was instrumental in understanding the business and religious foundations of Colorado Springs. This chapter is largely an application of Atkins' work to the Chambers' story, or an illustration of Atkins' points by the story of the Chambers family.

98

The motto of the state of Colorado is *"Nil Sine Numine,"* which is Latin for "Nothing Without the Deity," which perfectly sums up the centrality of religious sensibilities to Colorado Springs but also the generic nature of this ideal. Colorado Springs was a colony town, carefully planned and organized by the Colorado Springs Company—which was just that: a company, a business, intending to produce and sell a successful product. The men themselves used the language of founding a colony, a town set out for a particular purpose and carefully organized to attain a certain goal. The Colorado Springs Company's goal, which was originally envisioned by General William Palmer but largely carried out by General Robert Cameron and Major Henry McAllister, was to create a safe and stable wealthy resort town for the upper and middle classes. To cultivate this, Palmer, McAllister, and other boosters believed that the morality of Christianity was just as good for business as it was for the soul, thus they sought to infuse their new town with this Christian ethic from the very beginning.[226] A town with a reputation for strong morality would draw women and families, not just men, and thus create a lasting society.

The most obvious way that the Colorado Springs Company wrote Christian morality into the newborn Colorado Springs was through the temperance clause present in every land deed. The Colorado Springs Company owned all the city land that it planned, plotted, and sold to settlers and businessmen. Every deed required landowners to sign to the agreement "that intoxicating liquors shall never be manufactured, sold, or otherwise disposed of, as a beverage, in any place of public

[226] Atkins, 80. It was not the Gospel itself, but a way of living in keeping with traditional Christian ideals that the Colorado Springs Company wanted to cultivate, attract, and spread. They saw that solutions to many typical Western problems could be found if the populace would live according to general Christian standards of responsible, self-controlled, and honest behavior. Because outward behavior, not heart change, was what the boosters cared about, and because it was not restricted to one denomination, I refer to this concept throughout as "generic Christian morality." This serves to show how the boosters led the town into blurring the lines between "business sense and souls," as Atkins puts it, so that it is hard to tell what apparently religious acts in early Colorado Springs are based upon regenerated hearts and what is done because they make for a lasting town.

resort, in or upon the premises hereby granted."[227] Though the deed did not outlaw the consumption of alcohol, it prohibited the production and sale of it on every piece of land inside city limits. In further explaining this requirement, the city directory added that "Provision was also made in all deeds that if these conditions were violated, the land and buildings thereon should revert to the original owners."[228] One business owner who violated this law and found his property confiscated challenged the regulation in 1873, suing and appealing all the way to the United States Supreme Court, which in 1880 upheld the Colorado Springs Company's temperance clause.[229] Colorado Springs, it seems, would be a dry town.

At first glance, many attributed this provision to Palmer's Quaker upbringing and assumed him to be a thoroughgoing teetotaler. In reality, the motivation for such a clause in the colony's founding was both more general and more complex. In founding Colorado Springs, Palmer did not work alone, nor did he neglect to consider the failures and successes of other Colorado towns and colonies. The temperance clause was copied from the Greeley Colony, a settlement north of Denver where General Robert Cameron and Nathan Meeker had seen success in fending off the usual immoralities and instabilities of western towns by forbidding the sale and production of liquor.[230] Palmer made no attempt to claim the temperance clause as his own original idea. Instead, he wrote

> The liquor restriction had already been adopted by Mr. Meeker for his
> Greeley colony. In the early summer of 1871, while we were making
> arrangements with General Cameron and some of his confreres to interest
> themselves in our new enterprise, I was asked by them whether we would
> adopt a similar restriction for the proposed Fountain colony [later

---

[227] *Directory of Colorado Springs,* (Colorado Springs: The Gazette Printing Company, 1896), 58, as well as *Directory of Colorado Springs, Manitou Springs, and Colorado City, for 1888,* (Colorado Springs: S.N. Francis, Printer, 1888), 60.

[228] *Directory of Colorado Springs, 1896,* 58.

[229] Atkins, 84.

[230] Ibid.

Colorado Springs]. Having had some experience with the railroad towns of the day in the new West, especially those whose generally short but always lively existence punctuated the successive stages of advance westward by the Kansas Pacific and Union Pacific railroads, I answered Yes.[231]

The idea of a temperance town initially had far more to do with business than with religious convictions. Palmer had no moral objection against liquor itself, as archeological evidence on his property proves.[232] Yet he and the other founders had seen what saloon-riddled frontier towns became. Ale-full railroad towns were boom and bust, destroying people's respectability and families' livelihoods along with them. The founders of the Colorado Springs Company wanted their colony to run as a successful and lasting business, attracting steady and upright citizens and well-to-do visitors.

Yet the religious sensibilities of such a decision could not be thoroughly separated from this business decision, nor did anyone make any attempt to do so. Discerning the motive behind these actions today is complex because the colony's leaders and boosters intentionally mixed capitalist and Christian motivations.[233] By advertising itself as an extremely upstanding Christian community, the colony would not only attract settlers, it would attract the kind of citizens the company wanted. If it could draw many people committed to upholding this generic Christian morality—hardworking, honest, and temperate individuals—the town would be a lasting success. Temperance alone, however, would not hold a town together. The Colorado Springs Company knew they needed something deeper than just land deeds to hold people to this standard of upright behavior. To hold

[231] Wilbur Fisk Stone, ed, *History of Colorado, Volume I,* (Chicago: The S. J. Clarke Publishing Company, 1918), 165.

[232] In 2018, Colorado Springs City Archeologist Anna Cordova discovered what was apparently a trash site for Palmer's Glen Eyrie. In excavating the site, Cordova and her team discovered enough wine and liquor bottles to ascertain that Palmer by no means abstained from serving or drinking alcohol himself. With Colorado City—which was not part of Colorado Springs and had no such temperance requirement—just down the street, it would not have been difficult for him to acquire the drink.

[233] Atkins, 80.

the people to their temperance commitments, the new citizens of Colorado Springs would need spiritual and moral shepherds. How could a Western town acquire pastors? Offering free land to churches was another method of both attracting citizens and bettering the town, and it succeeded in bringing in pastors and churches to help maintain the order the town needed.[234] Again, this was not a unique Colorado Springs Company idea, but that does not mean it was ineffective in bringing churches to the town. An 1874 map of Colorado Springs that the boosters spread far and wide marks four churches on its streets: Methodist, Baptist, Presbyterian, and Episcopal.

By 1879, at least twelve churches could be found in Colorado Springs, representing "all the principle [sic] religious denominations:" Baptists, Presbyterians, Methodists, Episcopalians, Congregationalists, Methodist Episcopalians, Unitarians, and Catholics.[235] Sometimes multiple congregations met in the same building, but in less than ten years Colorado Springs had succeeded in winning itself many churches by its gifts of free land. The map on the following page, Figure 32, names and numbers the churches as a way of showing off the religious sensibilities of the town to potential settlers.

---

[234] Atkins, 85. Not every church was included in this generosity. Though the Colorado Springs Company provided property free of charge to many Protestant churches, the Catholic church had to buy its own land for a building. This unfairness is typical of the period. Protestants had long been suspicious of Catholics. As large numbers of Irish Catholic immigrants settled in America in the late 1800s, many White Anglo-Saxon Americans stereotyped Irish immigrants as drunk, lazy, and disorderly—not the kind of settler which the United States in general and in Colorado Springs in particular wanted to attract. Many Americans discriminated against Catholics as a way to keep out immigrants as well.

[235] *Colorado Springs, Manitou, and Colorado City [Colorado] Directory: 1879-1880* (Colorado Springs: Tribe and Jefferay, Printers, Binders, and Stationers, 1879), 32-35.

102

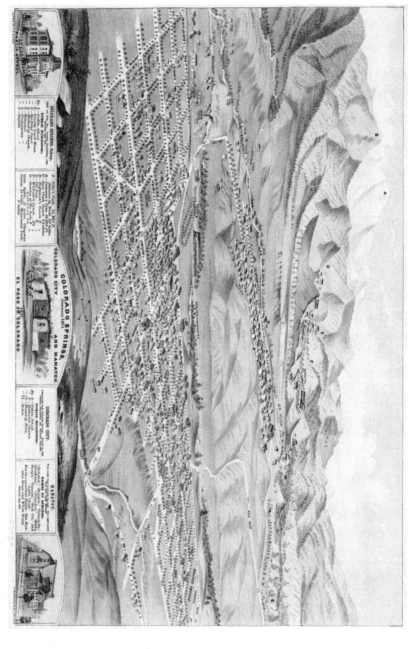

Figure 32 - 1874 map of Colorado Springs. From the Library of Congress.

Like the temperance clause, free land for churches was a double-edged sword to fulfill the goal of creating and maintaining an anti-frontier town. Churches would draw the right kind of citizens and improve the character of the ones who were there. Rather than just rugged single men seeking adventure, a town like this would draw families eager to establish a steady home. It is no accident that promotional materials for Colorado Springs advertised the number of churches, such as in the map above. Those looking to move to Colorado but apprehensive about the rugged immorality of the West would find a town with multiple churches extremely attractive—and boosters wasted no time in boasting of this feature. Once people arrived, the churches would cultivate in them the morals and sensibilities that would lead them to cooperate with and uphold the temperance clause of land deeds and even pursue further legislation that enforced Christian morality. For example, pastors worked with city leaders in developing the Sabbath laws that would prevent stores in town from conducting business on Sundays.[236] Churches were key to the development of Colorado Springs as an anti-frontier town.

The Chambers' church participation displays both sides of this religious boosterism. Robert and Elsie had lived within walking distance of the Buffalo Crossroads Methodist Episcopal church in Limestone, Pennsylvania, and were committed church members their whole lives. It is reasonable to speculate, therefore, that the Christian morals of the town were important factors in Robert Chambers' choice to make Colorado Springs the family's new home when he visited from Denver in early 1874.[237] By the time Robert visited the city, a Methodist Episcopal Church was already established. It was initially organized in 1871 and given a plot of land on Weber Street by the Colorado Springs Company,

---

[236] Atkins, 90.

[237] Mary Chambers DeLong, "The Chambers Family History," 3.

where it had a church building completed by April 1872.[238] By 1874 the church had
already completed an addition to its building, indicating a congregation that was
growing along with the city. When Robert Chambers settled his family in a house
in Colorado Springs that summer, they found themselves just five blocks north of
this church.[239] The Chambers obviously attended and were involved members at
this church soon after arriving in Colorado Springs.

The Chambers remained active and faithful church members and leaders even
after they moved out to Rock Ledge Ranch. The Ranch was a good five miles from
their church, and the early years on the Ranch were busy with building the house,
digging irrigation ditches, and fighting off grasshoppers. Nevertheless, the
Chambers did not neglect their church community. The offer of free "conveyance
to church" to their boarding guests attests that they were regular church attenders
themselves.[240] Furthermore, they certainly did more than just sit in a pew on
Sunday mornings. On December 30, 1876, the *Gazette* listed newly elected officers
of the Methodist Episcopal (or M.E.) Church of Colorado Springs. Robert is listed
as a new trustee (see Figure 33 on page 105).[241] As a trustee, Robert would have
had responsibilities in the care of church property and the handling of money in
the church. His election to such an important and prestigious position after less
than two years in the community indicates that he was well-known and respected

---

[238] Manly Dayton Ormes and Eleanor R. Ormes, *The Book of Colorado Springs* (Colorado Springs: The Dentan Printing Co, 1933), 197. The Chambers attended the First Methodist Episcopal Church, but of course it was not called that until there was a second Methodist Episcopal church. It apparently took up the title "first" between 1879 and 1882, perhaps when it moved locations. The church's first location was at Colorado Avenue and Weber Street, but in 1880 it bought a new plot on corner of Nevada and Kiowa, where the new building was completed in 1881.

[239] Elsie Chambers, "What Happened While the Cabin Lived," 5. Elsie records that the Chambers lived on the corner of Monument and Weber from May 1874 until February 1875.

[240] *The Colorado Mountaineer*, December 20, 1876. See page 53 for an image of this ad. A five-mile ride or drive to church from the Ranch would have taken approximately an hour by horse or horse and buggy.

[241] *Colorado Springs Gazette,* December 30, 1876.

by the congregation, considered both faithful and adept at handling important matters. Robert was reelected to this position in 1877, and the Colorado Springs Directories in 1879 and 1882 continue to list him as a trustee for the M.E.

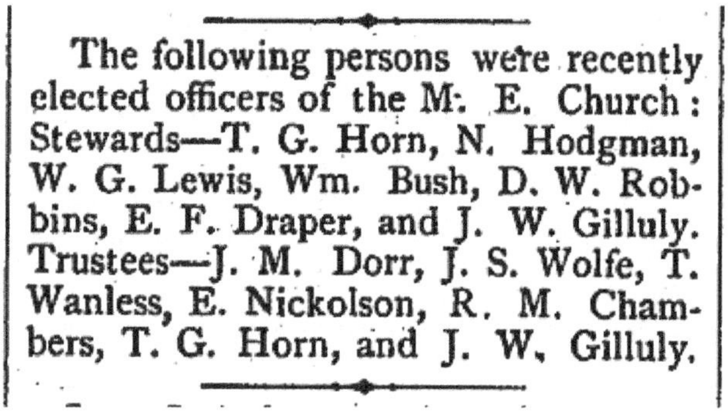

The following persons were recently elected officers of the M. E. Church: Stewards—T. G. Horn, N. Hodgman, W. G. Lewis, Wm. Bush, D. W. Robbins, E. F. Draper, and J. W. Gilluly. Trustees—J. M. Dorr, J. S. Wolfe, T. Wanless, E. Nickolson, R. M. Chambers, T. G. Horn, and J. W. Gilluly.

Figure 33 - Newly elected officers of the Methodist Episcopal Church, December 30, 1876.

Church.[242] The Chambers evidently took their Christianity seriously, reflecting the kind of citizens desired and serving the kind of religious community sought after by the boosters.

As the town grew, schoolhouses followed close behind the churches. In education as well as religion, the Chambers' story illustrates the kind of community the Colorado Springs Company was bent on creating. When they arrived in 1874, Benjamin "Bennie" Chambers was six years old. As Elsie Woolsey Chambers had attended Normal School in Bloomsburg, Pennsylvania, and afterwards worked as a teacher, and Robert had attended college classes himself, they would have taken their children's education very seriously.[243] In selecting their new home they would have looked for a community in which education would be prioritized. The boosters worked hard to attribute this characteristic to Colorado Springs, as can be seen in a speech given by Major McAllister in Figure 34. They knew that an

---

[242] *Colorado Springs Directory 1879*, 34, and *Colorado Springs Directory, 1882* (Colorado Springs: W.H.H. Raper and Co, Publishers, 1882), 25. In the directories after 1882 there is no longer room to list all the officers of every church as well as their addresses and service times. Robert Chambers may have and probably did remain a trustee beyond that year, but the directories cannot shed light on that question after 1882.

[243] Elsie is recorded as a student in Bloomsburg, PA, in the 1870 census, aged 25 years old. In Bloomsburg was the Bloomsburg Literary Institute, which was a state normal school (college for teachers). "United States Census, 1870", database with images. Elsie Woolsey in entry for Henry Carver, 1870. Elsie's granddaughter Grace DeLong notes that Elsie had "taught in Pennsylvania before her marriage." Grace DeLong, "A Ranch Begins: the Chambers Period, 1874-1900," 5.

106

upright, productive, and well-functioning society would require first-rate education for all ages. Almost at once the founders of Colorado Springs involved themselves in setting up schools. General Palmer's wife, Queen Palmer, began teaching the first children of the colony as early as November 1871. The first Colorado Springs school met in a house, then in the newspaper office building. By 1874 the school employed five teachers

> I take it for granted, ladies and gentlemen that, like all other travelers, you would like to hear something of the history of the places you visit. A very few words touching Colorado Springs may therefore be of interest to you. As late as the Summer of 1871, the site of the town through which you were driven this morning was the favorite feeding ground of many herds of timid antelope. [Applause.] The first stake of the surveyor was driven thereon on the first day of August, 1871. I will not trouble you with the details of its growth, we have given you an opportunity to see it for yourselves. You have seen its churches, school houses, stores, banking establishments, and hundreds of neat dwellings, the homes of between three and four thousand people of as high a standard of morality and intelligence as can probably be found in any community in the United States. [Great applause.] Nor is it, ladies and gentlemen, as its name might imply, merely the home

Figure 34 - The Colorado Springs Gazette, March 11, 1876, records a speech from Major Henry McAllister, in which he lists churches and schools first in noting the development of the town.

instructing various grades in dispersed rooms across town as citizens raised money and built a schoolhouse. Because of the swiftly-growing population, the school buildings filled faster than they could be constructed, sometimes forcing classes to meet for only half-days in order to accommodate all the students.[244] Yet in typical Western spirit, they carried on and made do with what they had. Clearly the early settlers of Colorado Springs were just as interested in education as the colony's founders had been.

City directories later in the 1870s boasted that "the educational interests of the town are carefully attended to," and the newspapers agreed.[245] In February 1875 a *Gazette* reporter visited all the classes meeting in various locations around the town, describing the teachers, students, locations, and methods of instruction. "Bennie Chambers" is listed in the "Second Primary" class. This group, composed of fifty-

[244] Ormes, 141-143.

[245] *Colorado Springs Directory 1879*, 4.

eight five- to nine-year-olds, met for classes in a room near the intersection of Cascade Avenue and Cucharas Street.[246] The presiding teacher was a Miss E. J. Merritt, praised as "a lady who has had long experience in teaching." The reporter notes that the school teaches children by the "Phonic and Object methods." To explain this method, he describes it:

> during our visit they were being drilled on the words 'combustible' and 'inflammable,' the meaning of the words being conveyed to them by actual demonstration. The little folk are apt learners, and their attentions easily secured by this method of tuition.[247]

Clearly this was an experienced teacher, who knew that the best way to keep the attention of fifty-plus youngsters was to explode things or set them on fire. Though never stating this boast outright, the article contains the typical booster rhetoric, implying throughout that although they might not have a dedicated schoolhouse, the children of Colorado Springs were by no means being deprived of a good education.

The Chambers family not only took advantage of the education available in Colorado Springs, they also contributed to it. No records remain about where Ben, Eleanor, and Mary attended school in the first decade at Rock Ledge Ranch between 1875 and 1887. Perhaps this can be explained by the fact that Elsie was obviously very well qualified to teach the children herself, but still, no documents clarify the answer. Yet starting in 1888, clear records surface to show that Robert and Elsie began to invest in the education of their neighbors' children as well as their own. Official school board notes written in Mrs. Chambers' handwriting explain that the nearby families formed School District 35 in the Camp Creek Valley on January 6, 1888. With Robert as Chairman and Elsie as Secretary, the electors of this new district "moved that the west room of R.M. Chambers' house be rented for use as a school-room at $10.00 per month including stove, coal, and

---

[246] *Colorado Springs Gazette,* February 20, 1875.

[247] *Colorado Springs Gazette,* February 20, 1875.

blackboard."[248] Additionally, this school board consisting of the Chambers and their near neighbors established that the school would meet for five hours a day. It would begin in February and continue for three months.

The rent was not the only money the Chambers made from this educational endeavor in 1888. From March to May the receipts of the school board note that not only was Robert Chambers being paid rent for the school, but Elsie was being paid the teacher's salary—forty dollars a month (close to $1200 in 2020 dollars).[249] Some express surprise that Mrs. Chambers taught school as a married woman, but expansion in roles for women was common in the West. While some school districts in the nineteenth century did not permit teachers to be married, this was by no means a universal rule, even if it was a fairly common one. Colorado Springs had no such laws, as married women were some of the first teachers in the area. Different schools and school districts would decide this matter for themselves, and out West those hungry for "book-learning" would take whatever qualified teachers they could get. With teachers, just as with the location of schools, people did the best they could with what they had. They did not attempt to make things more difficult than necessary. Elsie Chambers was very well qualified, and the Chambers, as always, did not waste opportunities for service and entrepreneurship. Elsie's tenure as teacher in the Glen Eyrie School lasted less than a year, and by February 1889 there were plans for a separate school building on the Chambers property as well as a different teacher.[250]

---

[248] Glen Eyrie School District Record, Jan 12, 1888, in Carol Kennis Lopez, "Glenn Eyrie School and the Chambers Family," March 23, 1990. The seemingly small note about coal confirms an interesting fact as well: the Chambers heated their home with coal, which is established not only by this school board record but also by a coal receipt that was found in the walls of the Rock Ledge House when it was restored. The fireplaces in the house were small, intended for coal, and the front rooms of the house were heated by small coal heating stoves. Their large kitchen stove could use either wood or coal as fuel. Because of the shortage of trees in Colorado Springs when settlers arrived, coal was the main fuel for heat in those early years. There were many coal mines in the Colorado Springs area. Thus it is likely that the Chambers did all their heating with coal.

[249] Carol Kennis Lopez, "Glenn Eyrie School and the Chambers Family," March 23, 1990.

[250] Ibid.

Thus Elsie Chambers was set up as a schoolteacher in her own home for a time. The location of the schoolroom—"the west room" as it is described in the school board minutes—stands as a little bit of a mystery. The most western room in the Rock Ledge House is the kitchen. Although this would have provided a source of heat through the cold winter and spring, it is hard to imagine that this busy farmhouse kitchen would have been a convenient place for a school to be meeting. Perhaps the west room refers to the back parlor or informal parlor. This is a decently spacious, well-lit room with a west-facing window that could hold a small class. However, Grace DeLong wrote that school was held "in an upstairs bedroom," adding a further layer of complication.[251] None of the upstairs bedrooms are truly west-facing, as the roof slopes down dramatically on the west side of the second floor. There is, perhaps, one more option, though it seems far-fetched. The steep, narrow staircase in the kitchen led to the bedrooms upstairs through a small, dark room on the west side of the second story of the house. This room at one point had a dormer window, meaning it could have had natural light and enough room to stand. Yet at the same time, the room is narrow and the roof is so steep that it does not seem like it could have held much of a classroom. Perhaps someday the true identity of "the west room of R.M. Chambers house" will be discovered. For now, it remains a mystery. Wherever school was held, it is well-established by both Chambers family history and school records that the school met in the Rock Ledge House for at least several months until a building was constructed.

The Glen Eyrie School remained a whole-family endeavor for the Chambers even after the school no longer met in their home. The 1890 school board minutes note that Ben L. Chambers became the secretary, and then Robert Chambers took a turn as secretary temporarily in 1892.[252] After high school, Eleanor and Mary

---

[251] Grace DeLong, "A Ranch Begins: The Chambers Period 1874-1900," 5.

[252] Glen Eyrie School District Record, Jan 1890, in Carol Kennis Lopez, "Glenn Eyrie School and the Chambers Family," March 23, 1990. Lopez notes that the minutes in the years when Elsie was the secretary were very neat and thorough, but they become less and less legible as the secretaries changed.

Chambers each took turns teaching in this little school for a few terms. Eleanor taught from September 1892 until April 1893 and Mary taught for a year or two starting in 1893.[253] The family connection with the school extended beyond blood relatives to relations by marriage. May Kinney, who was the sister of Ben Chambers' wife (Madge Kinney), taught at the school and likely boarded with the Chambers. May Kinney appears in this picture of students, teacher, and schoolhouse. The photo is undated but from the clothing of the teacher and some of the students, it appears that it was taken some time in the 1890s.

Figure 35 - Writing on back of original image reads "Benj. L. Chambers. Teacher is May (Mamie) Kinney, Madge Kinney's sister and Dorothy Ellis Chambers Mother." Courtesy Bruce W. Dunbar Family Collection.

This is consistent with the school records, as two different young women with the last name of Kinney taught at the Glen Eyrie School in 1890-1892.[254] Far from

---

[253] Eleanor would have been nineteen or twenty years old at this time, and Mary would have been 18 when she began teaching in September. Glen Eyrie School District Record, September 1893, in Carol Kennis Lopez, "Glenn Eyrie School and the Chambers Family," March 23, 1990, and Grace DeLong, "A Ranch Begins: The Chambers Period 1874-1900," 6. Special thanks to Hillary Mannion for her help in searching the archives at the Colorado Springs Pioneers Museum.

[254] Glen Eyrie School District Record, 1892. From April 1890-December 1891, M.B. Kinney, and from January 1892-April 1892, E.D. Kinney.

simply benefiting from the push for education in this anti-frontier town, the Chambers actively pursued creating new opportunities for it. The Chambers family's involvement in teaching and administrating school during their years at Rock Ledge Ranch fits both their established character and the character of the town they were now a part of. Always entrepreneurs, the Chambers did not miss an opportunity to work with their neighbors to serve their community and bring in income at the same time. Their commitment to starting and maintaining a school displays the spirit of Colorado Springs, attempting to be an anti-frontier town by promoting education.

It was not merely primary education that the Chambers and Colorado Springs at large were interested in, however. In the state of Colorado men of "missionary zeal and prayerful lives" were of the opinion that there must be a college in which leaders of strong moral character could be trained.[255] In early 1874, the ministers who sought to create this institution decided on Colorado Springs as the location for the college. Among the prominent men named to its board of trustees were some of Colorado Springs' usual suspects: Henry McAllister Jr., General William J. Palmer, and Dr. William A Bell.[256] This idea for a college fit in beautifully with the plans for cultivating a moral citizenry in Colorado Springs, and the Colorado Springs Company gave 160 acres for the school, which quickly dropped "Springs" from its name to become, simply, "Colorado College."[257]

The college succeeded in bringing a moral reputation to the town from the start. Reverend Jonathan Edwards—the great-grandson of the famous pre-Revolutionary War pastor and theologian Jonathan Edwards—became the first president (and initially, the only professor) of the college, which began its first term on May 1, 1874. Like the public schools, the college met in various buildings as it waited for its own to be built. It was not until 1880 that the first college building,

---

[255] Ormes, 160.

[256] Ibid., 160.

[257] Atkins, 85.

Palmer Hall (now called Cutler Hall) was completed.[258] In the mid-1880s, tuition cost thirty-five dollars (just over $800 in 2020 dollars) and there were anywhere from thirty to fifty students in attendance.[259] The college struggled somewhat through the 1870s and 1880s but was a thriving institution by the 1890s, as evidenced by the many activities of student clubs noted in the school paper, the *Colorado Collegian*.

The Chambers story intersects with Colorado College as well. Though there were many other probable factors that caused Robert Chambers to "fall in love" with Colorado Springs in April 1874, the promise of a college was likely a very attractive prospect. If nothing else, it was another solid piece of evidence that boosters could present to show that Colorado Springs was an excellent place to raise a family. It appears that at least Eleanor (and likely the other Chambers children) took advantage of opportunities for education at the college during their years at the Ranch. Eleanor Chambers, who went on to pursue nursing school, began her medical career as a student at Colorado College. In the 1892 Colorado Springs city directory, she is listed as a medical student living at 723 North Weber, which would have been about a fifteen-minute walk from the main college building, which was Palmer Hall.[260] Tidbits of her college career can be scavenged from the pages of the *Colorado Collegian*, which published organization and club meeting times as well as essays, opinion pieces, and jokes from the student body. Eleanor, or "Nora" Chambers, evidently began taking college classes in October of 1890, and continued through at least May 1892, as evidenced by several editions of the *Colorado Collegian* (see Figure 37).[261] She was involved in the Minerva Literary

---

[258] Ormes, 160.

[259] Loe, *Life in the Altitudes*, 54.

[260] *Directory of Colorado Springs, Colorado City, and Manitou for 1892* (Colorado Springs: The Republic Publishing Company, 1892), 76. Eleanor went on to nursing school at the Farrand Training School for Nurses at Harper's Hospital in Detroit, Michigan. She graduated with her nursing degree in 1897.

[261] *The Colorado Collegian*, October 1, 1890, and May 1, 1892.

Society, a club in which women met weekly to present and discuss essays on poetry and prose. Colorado College had at least three such literary societies in 1892.

> **Miss Nora Chambers, formerly of the High School, has entered the Middle Preparatory class this year.**

Figure 36a - The Colorado Collegian, October 1, 1890. Eleanor moves from high school into college.

> **Miss Alice Bacon and Miss Nora Chambers have been initiated into the mysteries of the Minerva.**

Figure 37b - The Colorado Collegian, May 1, 1892. Eleanor joins the Minerva Society.

Mary Chambers may also have attended some classes at the college. In the 1896 city directory she is listed as a stenographer living at 529 E. Willamette (the same address is listed for Robert and Elsie Chambers).[262] It is likely that Mary took a stenography course at Colorado College in order to learn those skills.[263] The years of hard work at Rock Ledge Ranch enabled the Chambers to ensure their girls received education beyond high school and could do it from conveniently close in the city.

Colorado College fit perfectly into the Colorado Springs Company's strategy of cultivating generic Christian morality. The very presence of the college was an asset in the promotion of Colorado Springs as an anti-frontier town, but it offered a further benefit. A congregational liberal arts college would train leaders of strong ethical character to lead the town in a stable direction. It was committed to Christianity and yet explicitly nondenominational—the second president of the

---

[262] *Directory of Colorado Springs,* 1896, 77. Apparently the Chambers moved around in town, as the town addresses recorded for them are not all the same.

[263] Eleanor Chambers is not the only connection between Rock Ledge Ranch and Colorado College. After General Palmer acquired the property from the Chambers family, he built a house on it for his half-sister-in-law, Charlotte Sclater, and her husband William. William Sclater was an ornithologist who curated the natural history museum at Colorado College during the two years he and his wife lived in the Orchard House at Rock Ledge Ranch.

114

college, Reverend James Dougherty, described the college as "distinctly and definitely a Christian College, yet the institution is not sectarian, not theological, not under any ecclesiastical control."[264] Like the churches, Colorado College was intended to help cultivate morals in the citizens of Colorado Springs, raising up leaders that would maintain a stable religious ethic. The professors and students of the college became essential in the religious life of the town through their active involvement in church and ecumenical organizations. The college brought moral training and the prospect of sophistication to this town that was seeking to appear as little like the rough-and-tumble mining towns as possible.

While churches and schools proved important in the cultivation of an upright and attractive city, even more powerful in maintaining this image and reality were ecumenical organizations. Religious organizations working toward social reform had been springing up in the United States since the Second Great Awakening in the first quarter of the nineteenth century. Many of these organizations did not exclude on the basis of church denominations. They found strength in numbers as they were able to gain more workers and reach more people if they were ecumenical—different denominations of churches banding together over one mutual concern. This kind of unity of purpose in universal Christianity was exactly the environment the boosters were trying to create. Although in the first decade of the city, boosters were far more focused on churches and schools, ecumenical organizations began to develop in the late 1870s and by the late 1880s were essential to town life.

Three of the most influential ecumenical organizations in Colorado Springs were the Ministerial Association, the Associated Charities, and the Young Men's Christian Association (YMCA). The Ministerial Association organized pastors to lobby for stricter adherence to morality in the town's laws, pushing for enforcement of Sabbath-breaking and gambling laws, among other misbehaviors.[265] A group of women formed the Associated Charities in 1875 in

---

[264] Ormes, 162.

[265] Atkins, 90.

order to help the deserving poor and sick who came to Colorado Springs for the climate cure. Boosters quickly discovered that their proclamations about the salubrious effects of the climate brought the poor as well as the rich, despite warnings that fat pockets were necessary for the cure. The Associated Charities sought to help those who could become upright and contributing citizens. Their help, therefore, depended on whether they judged the needy to be the kind of people they wanted to remain in the city.[266] The YMCA, established in Colorado Springs in 1878, provided community, activities, and space for hosting events. Its mission to promote "the spiritual, intellectual, social and physical welfare of young men" aligned it with the commitment to generic Christian morality that the whole town was pursuing.[267] Like the other organizations, the YMCA grew stronger as the turn of the century drew closer. These are only the largest three of the many Christian associations; by 1900 at least twelve ecumenical organizations existed to educate, support, and enforce the morality that the town based its business on. These organizations included the Young Women's Christian Association, the Sunday School Union, the Christian Endeavor Union, the Anti-Cigarette League, the Anti-Saloon League, the Prohibition League, and the Woman's Christian Temperance Union.[268]

The Woman's Christian Temperance Union (WCTU) was a nationwide ecumenical organization that was growing rapidly between 1875 and 1900, and it is here that the Chambers once again showed themselves to be exemplary citizens of Colorado Springs. Mrs. Chambers was an active member and leader in the Woman's Christian Temperance Union during and after her years at Rock Ledge Ranch, but the Union itself deserves a little backstory.

In December 1873, hordes of women in the Midwest stormed bars singing and praying in an attempt to stop the sale and consumption of alcohol.[269] The

---

[266] Atkins, 87.

[267] Ibid., 89.

[268] Ibid., 86.

temperance movement had long focused on stopping the abuse of alcohol in order to protect the family. Perceiving that drunk husbands and fathers abused wives and mothers, they stepped up to change that, believing that by changing the hearts of both drunkards and barkeepers they could save the family from much sorrow and suffering. When they realized that their temperance crusades did not have lasting effect, they sought a different way: an organization that could exert continual influence to effect change. In November 1874 women from sixteen states met at a national convention to form the Woman's Christian Temperance Union. Under the leadership of President Annie Wittenmyer, the WCTU spent the first five years of its existence working with the philosophy of gospel temperance, which aimed to reform alcoholics and liquor sellers by conversion to Christianity.[270] The WCTU began to involve itself in other reform efforts like prison reform, but it generally stayed close to the temperance topic.

In 1879, however, Frances Willard was elected the next president of the WCTU, and she revolutionized the scope and mission of the Union. The WCTU and America at large saw temperance as a way to wield women's moral and spiritual influence to protect women, children, and the home from poverty and violence. The women's sphere had already been broadening to include many social reforms it had not touched fifty years before; Willard set out to push the bounds of that sphere even further. Having been frustrated since childhood by the way she felt the culture limited females to what they considered womanly pursuits, Willard believed the best way for women to gain more independence and autonomy was to have direct political power. Desiring that women have the vote, she managed to connect this issue to temperance by arguing that to effectively protect their homes, women ought to have a voice in their communities. At first, this idea was limited to a woman having a say in the legality of alcohol in her community, but Willard and

---

[269] Jack S. Blocker, *"Give to the Winds Thy Fears:" The Women's Temperance Crusade, 1873-1874* (Westport, Connecticut: Greenwood Press, 1985), 33.

[270] Erin M. Masson, "The Women's Christian Temperance Union 1874-1898: Combating Domestic Violence," *William and Mary Journal of Women and the Law* 3, no. 1 (1997): 169-170.

the WCTU pushed it further under the name of "Home Protection" to advocate for total female suffrage.[271] To achieve this, however, Willard not only needed the support of her fellow WCTU members, she needed the support of the nation. The WCTU needed to spread. Willard travelled around the United States, speaking and founding local chapters of the WCTU everywhere from the deep South to the far West.[272] The Colorado Springs chapter of the WCTU was one of these chapters she founded during her western "round-up," an honor that the local chapter did

not soon forget (see Figure 117).[273] Once she had united women from across the country into the Union, she was presented with a larger task: how to keep these diverse women from many denominations and backgrounds working together toward a common goal.

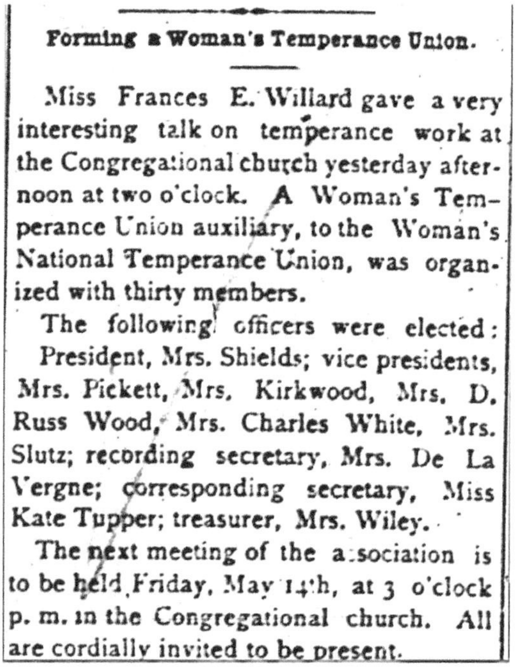

In 1881 Willard articulated the strategy to accomplish this task in her presidential address, declaring that to seek moral reform the WCTU must "Do Everything."[274] This quickly came to mean that each local chapter of the WCTU

Forming a Woman's Temperance Union.

Miss Frances E. Willard gave a very interesting talk on temperance work at the Congregational church yesterday afternoon at two o'clock. A Woman's Temperance Union auxiliary, to the Woman's National Temperance Union, was organized with thirty members.

The following officers were elected: President, Mrs. Shields; vice presidents, Mrs. Pickett, Mrs. Kirkwood, Mrs. D. Russ Wood, Mrs. Charles White, Mrs. Slutz; recording secretary, Mrs. De La Vergne; corresponding secretary, Miss Kate Tupper; treasurer, Mrs. Wiley.

The next meeting of the association is to be held Friday, May 14th, at 3 o'clock p. m. in the Congregational church. All are cordially invited to be present.

Figure 37 - Colorado Springs Gazette, May 1, 1880. Frances Willard organizes Colorado Springs WCTU.

could decide for itself what reforms to spearhead to serve its own community.

[271] Ruth Bordin, *Frances Willard: A Biography* (Chapel Hill: University of North Carolina Press, 1986), 100.

[272] Ruth Bordin, *Woman and Temperance: The Quest for Power and Liberty, 1873-1900* (American Civilization. Philadelphia: Temple University Press, 1981), 85.

[273] Ormes, 307.

[274] Bordin, *Frances Willard*, 130.

Under the banner of the WCTU, women could unite to pursue public reforms in whatever way suited their city, as long as it could somehow be related back to women, children, or the home. For example, in mining towns in Colorado, this often meant providing women with an escape from prostitution and teaching them a new trade to support themselves. In other places, women started kindergartens, helped young women find lodging in big cities, lobbied for legislation to protect women from assault, and more. In this way, Willard broadened the women's sphere to include even political functions, expanding into a realm long seen as unfit for women. Eventually, this entrance of women into wider and wider spheres led to a more universal acceptance of women's involvement in politics, including voting.

This expansion into politics, too, can be seen in the story of the Chambers family. In 1898, five years after the state of Colorado granted women the right to vote, Elsie Woolsey Chambers ran for the position of state auditor in Colorado as the candidate of the Prohibition party. She did not win the election, but neither was she last among the five candidates in the running (see Figure 39).[275]

Elsie's experience in the Union was likely a large factor in her having not only the interest and knowledge but also the skill to make it so far in

FOR AUDITOR OF STATE.
George S. Adams, R 2,615
Elsie W. Chambers, P 197
George W. Temple, F 4,015
Christian Miller, S 117
John A. Wayne, S. R 885

Temple's plurality 1,400

Figure 38 - Gazette November 24, 1898. Elsie W. Chambers as a candidate for Colorado State Auditor.

politics. This shows that Willard's "Do Everything" strategy mobilized an army of women across the country to reform their communities with a generic Christian morality under the aegis of the national Woman's Christian Temperance Union.

---

[275] *The Elbert County Banner,* November 4, 1898, *The Georgetown Courier,* November 12, 1898, *The Colorado Chieftain,* November 24, 1898.

The WCTU fit beautifully as the kind of organization that would ensure Colorado Springs kept its upright culture for years to come.

Amid all the farming, boarding, teaching, and organizing that kept her busy in the late 1880s and 1890s, Elsie W. Chambers was also serving her community on the state and local level through the Woman's Christian Temperance Union. Elsie's descendants remember her as being very involved with the WCTU, and external records attest that this is accurate. By October of 1889 she was putting her skill with word and pen to use for the WCTU. Her name appears in *The Salida Mail* newspaper as a member of the Committee On Constitution, representing the Colorado Springs Union. That same paper also includes an article she wrote in her role as "Press Superintendent" who recorded the happenings of that evening's meeting.[276] Clips from both of these newspapers can be seen in Figures 40 and 41 on page 120.

---

[276] *The Salida Mail,* October 11, 1889.

W. C. T. U.

For God and Home and Native Land

[This Column is Edited by the W. C. T. U.]

The annual state convention of the Women's Christian Temperance Union convened at 3 o'clock on Tuesday, September 24, at Fort Collins. Devotional exercises were conducted by Mrs. E. F. Leonard. Visiting members were given all the privileges of the convention possible to grant them.

The following committees were appointed by the chair:

On Credentials—Mrs. L. N. McIntyre and Mrs. Leonard of Denver.

On Resolutions—Mrs. Hicks, recently of Wyoming, now of Denver, Mrs. Beach, of Denver, Mrs. Hayward, formerly of Colorado Springs, now of Longmont, Mrs. Annis, now of Greely, and Mrs. M. D. Wilson, of Pueblo.

Plan of Work—Mrs. J. S. Sperry, of Pueblo, Mrs. Shapleigh, of Denver, Mrs. E. Smith, formerly of Leadville, Mrs. Eva Higgins, of La Veta, Mrs. E. F. Leonard and Mrs. M. Sprague, of Denver.

On Constitution—Mrs. E. W. Chambers, of Colorado Springs, Mrs. Cassell and Mrs. Brazee, of Denver, Mrs. T. M. Wallace, of Boulder, and Mrs. S. E. Fugard, of Pueblo.

Adjourned.

Figure 40 – Above. The Salida Mail newspaper, October 11, 1889. Mrs. E.W. Chambers of Colorado Springs is mentioned as appointed to the Committee On Constitution.

Figure 39 – Right. The Salida Mail newspaper, October 11, 1889. A piece written by E.W. Chambers, Press Superintendent.

TUESDAY EVENING.

At the evening session there was good singing, and Mrs. Brazee presided.

Words of welcome were given by Mrs. H. J. Furness, president of the Fort Collins union, Rev. J. S. Hamilton, of the Presbyterian church, and Rev. E. N. Elton, of the Baptist.

Mrs. Eva Higgins, of the southern district, responded with well chosen sentiments.

Mrs. Teedor, of Denver, favored the audience with a solo, after which the state president gave her annual address, opening with a Christian woman's tribute to Christianity and all it means to women.

Mrs. Leavitt and Miss Ackerman, our round the world missionaries, one after the other going alone on their lonely journey, were given words of appreciation and sympathy. The Loyal Legion in Denver reporting one child in attendance the first meeting, has grown to a membership of 160, who have taken the triple pledge against the use of alchoholic liquors, tobacco and profanity. The Christian Endeavor society was highly commended for its movement toward making amusements something more than amusement without intellectual development.

The Cottage home has received more systematic help from the unions the last year than ever before.

The departments of mothers' meetings and evangelical work were specially emphasized as important to be furthered with yet more zeal; also the press and literature departments were urged to be more energetically presented by the local unions as very effectual means of advancing the cause of temperance.

E. W. CHAMBERS,
Press Superintendent.

By 1896, Elsie had risen to the role of president of the Colorado Springs WCTU chapter, which met weekly in her church, the First M.E. Church on Nevada and Kiowa.[277] The directories reveal that in these years, the WCTU met in the YMCA reading room until at least 1894, then moved to meeting in churches and homes when that space became unavailable.[278] As president, Elsie again attended the state gathering of the WCTU, participating in a conference with the state president and local presidents to plan the "work to be done during the coming year."[279] Her work was not confined to meetings within the WCTU, however. The same paper announced that WCTU women from the conference would be speaking on temperance at local churches, and stated that on the coming Sunday, "Mrs. Elsie W. Chambers of Colorado Springs will occupy the pulpit" in Corona Methodist Church.[280]

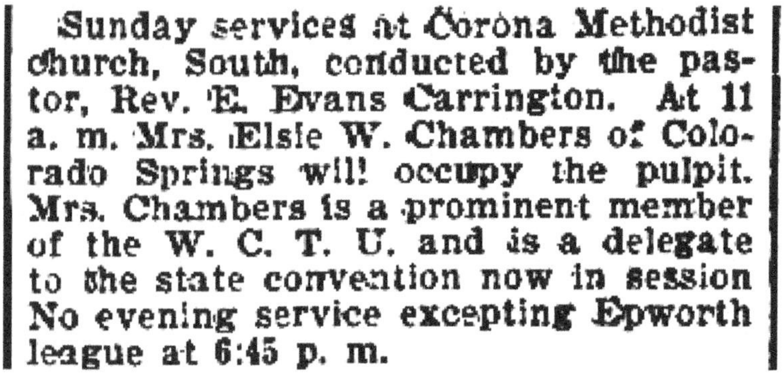

> Sunday services at Corona Methodist church, South, conducted by the pastor, Rev. E. Evans Carrington. At 11 a. m. Mrs. Elsie W. Chambers of Colorado Springs will occupy the pulpit. Mrs. Chambers is a prominent member of the W. C. T. U. and is a delegate to the state convention now in session No evening service excepting Epworth league at 6:45 p. m.

Figure 41 - Colorado Daily Chieftain, October 18, 1896.

Just fifty years previously, women speaking from the pulpit on behalf of reform efforts had split a group of determined women off from the abolition movement,

---

[277] *Directory of Colorado Springs,1896*, 23, 77. Not only is she listed as president in the directories section on the WCTU, she is listed later in the personal section as "Chambers, Mrs. E. W., president of W. C. T. U."

[278] *Colorado Springs City Directory, 1894*, 23.

[279] *Colorado Daily Chieftain*, October 18, 1896.

[280] Ibid.

122

motivating them to begin women's suffrage efforts. The Grimke sisters, speaking
out against slavery on Sunday mornings, were rejected by many abolitionists for
their rebellion against church tradition by speaking from the pulpit. It is remarkable
that the WCTU had allowed women to assume the speaking position in the church
that had resulted in their being cut off from reform efforts half a century before.
To be sure, the West was typically faster to adapt to new and more progressive
ways than the East—but women speaking from the pulpit on a Sunday morning
was quite a step. It is clear from what the newspapers tell us about Elsie that the
WCTU was making great strides towards expanding women's roles and rights in
Colorado. Described as "a prominent member of the W.C.T.U.," Elsie was clearly
skilled with more than just the written word, and was a valuable asset to the
Colorado WCTU.

In a town where making or selling alcohol was prohibited on every land deed,
however, what could the WCTU do? The Colorado Springs chapter displayed the
broadness of the "Do Everything" policy in the years that Elsie W. Chambers was
active in it. The Union promoted temperance through literature and education in
schools, held mothers' meetings, and organized weekly religious and educational
services for the local prison. Additionally, like many other Colorado WCTUs, the
Colorado Springs chapter also organized a home for working girls, to give them a
safe place to live.[281] And of course, they encouraged men not to drink alcohol—for
the demon liquor could still be acquired elsewhere and brought home for
consumption, so there was always temperance work to be done.

Another important effort of the Colorado Springs WCTU in these years was
the founding of a Woman's Exchange.[282] In the WCTU's own words, the Woman's
Exchange was an organization set up "to furnish home employment to women

[281] Ormes, 308. On a related note though not directly connected to Mrs. Chambers' and the
Colorado Springs WCTU's work, Colorado City's WCTU (separate from the Colorado Springs
chapter) bought a building among the saloons that lined the street and started a reading room.
Colorado City, unlike Colorado Springs, did not have a temperance requirement and therefore had an
excessive number of saloons. Ormes, 185.

[282] Ormes, 307.

who are under the necessity of earning money and yet, owing to family cares or ill health, are unable to go out by the day or week."[283] This enabled women in need to make a living from their own homes while still caring for their children or their invalid husbands. From baked goods to crocheted neckties to picnic lunches, these women could stay home and ply whatever domestic trade they did best for extra income. Wealthy and middle-class women could also donate their work on behalf of those struggling to make ends meet. Like other Colorado Springs charities, this was organized with the understanding that the town housed many invalids and with the expectation that it would aid those who were the kind of moral citizens the city wanted to keep around.

Mrs. Elsie W. Chambers' involvement in the WCTU lasted well beyond her years at Rock Ledge Ranch. This picture of her in Figure 43, taken in 1910, shows her sporting the white ribbon that symbolized her membership in the WCTU.[284] She wrote for the WCTU newsletter as she and Robert travelled the country on vacation from 1900 to 1902. Apparently when they passed back through Colorado Springs in August

Figure 42 - Elsie Woolsey Chambers, 65 years old. 1910, Pasadena, California. Courtesy Bruce W. Dunbar Family Collection.

[283] *Colorado Springs Gazette,* September 25, 1892.

[284] The white ribbon is a symbol of the WCTU to this day. Members wore white ribbons as Elsie does in this picture and were called "White Ribboners" or the "White Ribbon Army."

1902, the "pioneers of the Colorado Springs WCTU" met at her house again for a reception.[285] She was also active in the Pasadena and Southern California WCTU, and she continued to be a prolific speaker and writer for the Union throughout her life. Elsie W. Chambers was truly living out what Colorado Springs boosters wanted to see in their citizens: commitment not just to temperance, but temperance as one brick in the foundation of a solidly moral and Christian society.

Several conclusions stand out as one examines the Chambers' involvement in their community through church, school, and the Woman's Christian Temperance Union. It is remarkable that in the midst of all their businesses, the Chambers were active participants in building up and cultivating Colorado Springs in the realms of church, education, and ecumenical organizations. Their service in their community was not limited to one sphere. They were exemplary citizens in all of the areas the boosters promoted. Furthermore, Elsie's involvement in the Woman's Christian Temperance Union shows that the Chambers' values were very like the ones Colorado Springs boosters chose for the town from the beginning. Like the Colorado Springs Company, the Chambers connected temperance to an orderly and moral society, and viewed the former as a way to pursue the latter. Finally, it is telling that each member of the family was involved in this story in some way. It was not just Elsie and Robert who displayed the culture of Colorado Springs. The entire family served their community in the realm of education. Their story tells the story of this anti-frontier town as it developed in the nineteenth century and how its values played out in the lives of those everyday people who called the town home. More than just being the kind of people the boosters wanted to attract, the Chambers were the kind of people that cultivated Colorado Springs into an upright and stable town like one might find back East. It was people like them, putting their faith into action with hard work, who enabled Colorado Springs to become the town the Colorado Springs Company had envisioned.

---

[285] *Colorado Springs Gazette,* August 2, 1902.

Conclusion

"A Modern People, At Least in Our Own Eyes"

Looking back across her years at Rock Ledge Ranch, Elsie Woolsey Chambers remarked in her account "What Happened While the Cabin Lived,"

> As the years have gone by since 1874, the homestead claim has grown
> more fruit and vegetables than any other ranch in El Paso County. With its
> six acres of asparagus, hundreds of apple trees and hundreds of cherry
> trees besides other fruit, its value has increased many fold and shown what
> even the apparent barren land, so near to the foothills, may become by
> patient persistent effort. The enterprises of the vicinity within the past
> decade have brought modern ways, and all the aspirations for the
> opportunities of eastern city life, including business, educational, and
> religious life. The last of the old land-marks [sic] is gone and we are a
> modern people, at least in our own eyes.[286]

Indeed, between 1870 and 1900 Colorado had experienced incredible transformation and rapid economic growth. It was brought by "modern people" like the Chambers family, who moved to the West in a new wave of settlers whose motivations, goals, and opportunities were distinct from those of their predecessors. This new wave that settled Colorado Springs were of a different stock than those who had initially settled Denver. They changed the direction of westward expansion, so it was no longer just physical expansion outward into unknown lands, but building up towns, culture, and community to last into the

---

[286] Elsie Chambers, "What Happened While the Cabin Lived," 6.

future. The Chambers' story demonstrates that the West was settled in waves of various kinds of settlers, all necessary but with very different roles.

Robert and Elsie W. Chambers, and their children Benjamin, Eleanor, and Mary, were not part of the initial wave of explorers, miners, or even homesteaders who began westward expansion, settling towns like Denver, Golden, and Central City. Colorado Springs was not among those towns—no settlement in the Pikes Peak region was able to sustain a steady population, let alone grow larger, until the railroad arrived in 1871. Settlers who constituted the first wave of westward expansion were a tough bunch. Whether explorers looking for adventure, miners seeking fortune, or pioneers in their covered wagons pursuing a dream, they endured a brutal trek through the wilderness. They gave up many Eastern comforts and benefits to live an arduous and dangerous life in the West—that is, if they could get there alive! Hardy and independent, these pioneers faced many trials, failure, and loss as they dispersed across the West. Nevertheless, they spread the American people across the continent. They expanded horizontally, if you will. They literally discovered the lay of the land. They discovered where the water was, which agricultural methods worked, and what kept their livestock alive. In homes built of sod, dug into the ground, or built out of whatever resources they had on hand, they withstood wind and hail, blizzard and drought, fire and flood. This first wave struggled, but they figured out how to survive in the West.

The Chambers, and really the entire town of Colorado Springs, represent a later wave, as do the settlers who founded the towns of Greeley and Longmont. With the presence of the railroad, they did not have to sacrifice as much. They could bring more with them—both in terms of physical goods and Eastern life and habits. This was only possible because the previous settlers had laid the tracks for them. Although compared to twenty-first century Americans they were still "roughing it" in many ways, their lives look easy compared to the previous wave of settlers'. Iron stoves, pump organs, and wallpaper were not part of Walter Galloway's story. Yet they could be part of the Chambers'. Furthermore, their motivations, financial standing, and eventual destination differed from the earlier wave. The Chambers, like many others, travelled west because of poor health. They arrived with plenty of money, and they joined a town that was already physically planned out.

More than just the circumstances that brought them West, however, the Chambers and this second wave also had a role that was distinct from the previous settlers. Sometimes they still had to struggle for survival, yes, but others had done so before them, so they knew it was possible and even in some cases how to do it. With the ground already broken, they took on a different task—putting down roots, making the West home, building community. They figured out how to build a society that would last. With a community around them, the Chambers were able to do more than just milk their dairy cows or maintain their orchard. What is remarkable about the Chambers story is that they exemplify so many of the developments that came with the second wave of settlers. With these pioneers, life in the West quickly grew to include more churches and schools, new agricultural technology and organizations, religious and social reform organizations, and more. They could be involved in more organizations because they did not have to leave as many modern developments behind. Thus, they were able to begin new and more developed societies in the West.

This would not have been possible without the work of the first pioneers who scoped out the land and learned how to survive. Settlers needed water, food, and shelter before they could start churches, schools, and charitable societies. Without this second wave of settlers like the Chambers family—people who came for their health or to start colleges or to conduct grand agricultural experiments—the West would not have been settled. Instead, it would have merely been explored, mapped, and sparsely populated. After expansion horizontally, the necessary next step was to expand the West vertically. The second wave of settlers put down roots, built up community, and promoted economic growth by attracting tourists and invalids. With the basics covered, these settlers could focus on more than just living from day to day. They could think about the future. More than just getting by on the land, they were building something that would last.

Denver was established by the first type of settler. Colorado Springs was founded by the second. Not every town in the West had both waves of pioneers. Without both waves, however, the West would not have been settled. America needed settlers such as Walter Galloway, squatting on the land and raising enough crops and livestock to survive, to begin the process. It also needed pioneers such as Robert and Elsie Chambers, putting up wallpaper and building greenhouses and starting schools. Sometimes the same individuals could transition from one kind of settler to another, but often a different person entirely was necessary to move a settlement on to become "modern," to bring both the desire and the ability to attain life like back East. The West needed eager pioneers who could rough it and survive on homesteads, and then it needed those who could catch up with them, bringing traditional culture and values as well as modern technology, uniting the people and turning homesteads into homes. This explains Elsie W. Chambers' comment about being "modern people, at least in their own eyes." Previous settlers had been focused on survival because they had no other option. The Chambers' generation of settlers, however, living with expanded community and developing technology, could broaden their efforts and work with more of an eye toward the future. Their work still loomed large before them and still required "patient, persistent effort," but they had the means, the vision, and the time to shape their new Western communities into places they wanted their children and grandchildren to inhabit.

Explorers, miners, and early homesteaders played crucial roles in settling the West. Without the people who gave up comfortable lives in the East to rough it in the West, no progress would have been made. Yet they could not complete the whole task themselves. It took a different kind of pioneer, one with a vision for a community, not just a desire for adventure, a pocket full of gold, or a self-sustaining homestead. The Chambers were not the covered-wagon-Oregon-trail-pioneers we typically picture when we think about the settlement of the West. In some ways, their lives seem easy compared to all the hardships the first settlers faced. Yet the Chambers' work still required determination and sacrifice, and they were no less necessary. Survival in the West was possible—what next? Robert and Elsie Chambers, and second-wave pioneers like them, had to answer that question. Their response was to expand vertically, putting down roots and branching out into community, building up their society economically, agriculturally, and religiously. In Elsie Woolsey Chambers' own words, they brought "all the aspirations for the opportunities of eastern city life, including business, educational, and religious life," and not only the aspirations, but the will and the discipline to make it happen. Without them, the settlement of the West could not have continued into the future. The Chambers family, "modern people, at least in their own eyes," built on their predecessors' work to construct a home that would endure—in their Rock Ledge House and the community of Colorado Springs as a whole. Now the stones of that home endure to tell their story for years to come.

Acknowledgements

Like everything the Chambers did at Rock Ledge Ranch, a work like this requires not only "patient persistent effort," but community. I could not have done this without an army of supporters and a slightly shorter list of coffee shops with free wifi and good tea lattes. If you're ever in Lovettsville, Virginia, go have a London Fog at Backstreet Brews.

First, I would like to thank those whose knowledge of and curiosity about the past helped me dig up more than I realized could be discovered about the Chambers and the world in which they lived. Melissa Keown, Lead Historical Interpreter at Rock Ledge Ranch, Lauren Dunbar, Robert and Elsie Chambers' great-granddaughter, and Eric Metzger, Executive Director at the McAllister House Museum, thank you. Thank you for all the time you spent answering my questions, pointing me in the right direction, helping me find resources, educating me on history I was not aware of, and getting excited with me about what I was learning. Thank you for sharing your time so generously with me. And thank you for helping me transition this work from a college paper to a book! I could not have done this without you. I also owe a great deal to Carol Kennis Lopez, former Ranch Manager at Rock Ledge Ranch, who gathered so many of the documents and resources that made this research possible.

Second, many thanks to my parents, Jim and Martha Borders, who carefully read over my chapters, pointed out when I used the same word eleven times on the same page (I'm still trying to figure out a different word for "different," Mom), corrected my verb tenses, discussed the big ideas, and helped me become a better writer throughout this process. Also, thank you for supporting my Rock Ledge

Ranch "habit" for over ten years, and for your constant encouragement through this process. I love you.

Third, this project would be nothing if not for the guidance, gentle correction, and generous encouragement of Dr. Robert Spinney, Professor of History and my thesis advisor at Patrick Henry College. Thank you for training me to write well. Thank you for teaching me what history is, and how to write it in a way is true, good, and beautiful. I have become the writer, the historian, and the Christian I am today because of you. You have humbly and eagerly exemplified seeking the truth and communicating it clearly, and you inspire others to do the same. Words just do not suffice to express my gratitude for your example, instruction, and mentorship.

Finally, I want to thank all my friends and acquaintances who have asked me about my thesis or just listened to me talk about it much longer than they probably wanted to hear when it came up in conversation. I would especially like to thank my Kindred Spirits at Patrick Henry College for your never-ending interest in hearing about it, even when I went on about the grasshoppers for weeks on end. You made it all worth it. Thank you.

Soli Deo Gloria.

Elizabeth Borders

July 2022

Bibliography

"1878 Tax Schedule of Real and Personal Property of R.M. Chambers." Chambers Family Records, property of Rock Ledge Ranch Historic Site, Colorado, Springs, Colorado.

"1879 Tax Schedule of Real and Personal Property of R.M. Chambers." Chambers Family Records, property of Rock Ledge Ranch Historic Site, Colorado, Springs, Colorado.

"1880 Tax Schedule of Real and Personal Property of R.M. Chambers." Chambers Family Records, property of Rock Ledge Ranch Historic Site, Colorado, Springs, Colorado.

"1884 Tax Schedule of Real and Personal Property of R.M. Chambers." Chambers Family Records, property of Rock Ledge Ranch Historic Site, Colorado, Springs, Colorado.

"1885 Tax Schedule of Real and Personal Property of R.M. Chambers." Chambers Family Records, property of Rock Ledge Ranch Historic Site, Colorado, Springs, Colorado.

Abbott, Carl, and Stephen J. Leonard and Thomas J. Noel. *Colorado: A History of the Centennial State, Fifth Edition.* Boulder, CO: University Press of Colorado, 2013.

Atkins, Gregory. "'Business Sense If Not Souls': Boosters and Religion in Colorado Springs, 1871-1909." *The Journal of the Gilded Age and Progressive Era* 17, no. 1 (2018): 77–97. doi:10.1017/S1537781417000561.

Brands, H. W. *Dreams of El Dorado: A History of the American West.* First ed. New York: Basic Books, 2019.

Blocker, Jack S. *"Give to the Winds Thy Fears:" The Women's Temperance Crusade, 1873-1874* Westport, Connecticut: Greenwood Press, 1985.

Bordin, Ruth. *Frances Willard: A Biography.* Chapel Hill: University of North Carolina Press, 1986.

Bordin, Ruth. *Woman and Temperance: The Quest for Power and Liberty, 1873-1900.* American Civilization. Philadelphia: Temple University Press, 1981.

Cayleff, Susan E. *Nature's Path: A History of Naturopathic Healing in America.* Baltimore, Maryland: Johns Hopkins University Press, 2016. https://search.ebscohost.com/login.aspx?direct=true&db=nlebk&AN=1 083530&site=ehost-live.

Chambers, Elsie Woolsey. "What Happened While The Cabin Lived." Unpublished manuscript, ca. 1885. Property of Rock Ledge Ranch Historic Site, Colorado, Springs, Colorado.

Colorado Historic Newspapers Collection, Colorado State Library, https://www.coloradohistoricnewspapers.org/.

Colorado Springs Directory, 1882. Colorado Springs: W.H.H. Raper and Co, Publishers, 1882.

Colorado Springs, Manitou, and Colorado City [Colorado] Directory: 1879-1880. Colorado Springs: Tribe and Jefferay, Printers, Binders, and Stationers, 1879.

"Colorado State Census, 1885," database with images. *FamilySearch* https://familysearch.org/ark:/61903/1:1:K8WF-WP7: 4 March 2021. Robt Chamber, 1885; citing NARA microfilm publication M158 (Washington, D.C.: National Archives and Records Administration, n.d.); FHL microfilm 498, 506.

"Colorado State Census, 1885," database with images. *FamilySearch* (https://familysearch.org/ark:/61903/3:1:939N-F4LS-J?cc=1807096&wc=M83M-B3D%3A149197101%2C149204801%2C149196702 : 20 May 2014), El Paso > 3 > Agriculture > image 4 of 5; citing NARA microfilm publication M158 (Washington D.C.: National Archives and Records Administration, n.d.).

Daniel, Thomas M. *Captain of Death: The Story of Tuberculosis*. Rochester, NY, USA: University of Rochester Press, 1997. https://search-ebscohost-com.ezproxy.phc.edu/login.aspx?direct=true&db=nlebk&AN=24917&sit e=ehost-live.

DeLong, Grace. "A Ranch Begins: The Chambers Period, 1874-1900." Unpublished manuscript. Property of Rock Ledge Ranch Historic Site, Colorado, Springs, Colorado.

DeLong, Mary Chambers. "Chambers Family History." Unpublished manuscript. Property of Rock Ledge Ranch Historic Site, Colorado, Springs, Colorado.

Denver and Rio Grande Railway Company. *Health, Wealth, and Pleasure in Colorado and New Mexico*. A Centennial Ed. Santa Fe: Museum of New Mexico Press, 1980.

Denver Library Digital Collection. (n.d.). *CG4310 1862 .C3*. CONTENTdm. Retrieved June 27, 2022, from https://digital.denverlibrary.org/digital/collection/p16079coll39/id/39/rec/89

Directory of Colorado Springs, Colorado City, and Manitou for 1892. Colorado Springs: The Republic Publishing Company, 1892.

Directory of Colorado Springs. Colorado Springs: The Gazette Printing Company, 1896.

Dunbar, Lauren. "Coming to Colorado 1874." Rock Ledge Ranch Annunciator, June 2021.

Dunbar, Robert G. "Agricultural Adjustments in Eastern Colorado in the Eighteen-Nineties." *Agricultural History* 18, no. 1 (1944): 41–52. http://www.jstor.org/stable/3739506.

Fraser, Caroline, ed. *Laura Ingalls Wilder: The Little House Books*. New York: HarperCollins Publishers, Inc., 2012.

Gondran, Gretchen A. "Declining Mortality in the United States in the Late Nineteenth and Early Twentieth Centuries." *Annales de Démographie Historique,* 1987. https://www.persee.fr/doc/adh_0066-2062_1988_num_1987_1_1686

Gulliford, Andrew. "Come Only if Rich: The health-seeker movement in Colorado Springs,". Collection CU 83. Special Collections, Pikes Peak Library District.

Hill, Pamela Smith, editor. *Pioneer Girl: The Annotated Autobiography*. Pierre, South Dakota: South Dakota Historical Society Press, 2014.

Hopkins, Theodore L. Extinction of the Rocky Mountain Locust. *BioScience*, Volume 55, Issue 1, January 2005, Pages 80–81. https://doi.org/10.1641/0006-3568(2005)055[0080:EOTRML]2.0.CO;2

Howe, Barbara J. *Houses and Homes: Exploring Their History*. The Nearby History Series, 2. Nashville, TN.: American Association for State and Local History, 1987.

Howbert, Irving. *Memories of a Lifetime in the Pike's Peak Region*. Glorieta, N.M: Rio Grande Press, 1970.

Kennis, Carol. "Glenn Eyrie School and the Chambers Family." Unpublished manuscript, 1990.

Leonard, Stephen J., and Thomas J. Noel. *A Short History of Denver*. Reno, Nevada: University of Nevada Press, 2016.

Loe, Nancy E. *Life in the Altitudes: An Illustrated History of Colorado Springs*. 1st ed. Woodland Hills, Calif.: Windsor Publications, 1983.

Lopez, Carol Kennis. "Agricultural Legacy: Rock Ledge Ranch Historic Site." Unpublished manuscript, 2017.

Masson, Erin M. "The Women's Christian Temperance Union 1874-1898: Combating Domestic Violence," William and Mary Journal of Women and the Law 3, no. 1 (1997). https://scholarship.law.wm.edu/cgi/viewcontent.cgi?referer=&httpsredir=1&article=1273&context=wmjowl.

Noel, Thomas J, Paul F Mahoney, and Richard E Stevens. *Historical Atlas of Colorado*. Norman: University of Oklahoma Press, 1993.

Ormes, Manly Dayton, and Eleanor R. Ormes. *The Book of Colorado Springs*. Colorado Springs: The Dentan Printing Co, 1933.

Pabor, William Edgar. *Fruit Culture in Colorado: A Manual of Information*. Denver: W.E. Pabor, Publisher, 1883.

Riley, Charles V. "Important Observations on the Rocky Mountain Locust, or 'Grasshopper' Pest of the West." *Scientific American* 36, no. 17 (1877): 260–61. http://www.jstor.org/stable/26057375.

"Rock Ledge Ranch Historic Site at Garden of the Gods." Accessed April 28, 2022. https://rockledgeranch.com.

Sklar, Kathryn Kish. "All Hail to Pure Cold Water!" *American Heritage* 26, no. 1 (1974).

Stone, Wilbur Fisk ed. *History of Colorado, Volume I*. Chicago: The S. J. Clarke Publishing Company, 1918.

"United States Census, 1870", database with images, <i>FamilySearch</i> (https://www.familysearch.org/ark:/61903/1:1:MZGZ-BKN : 29 May 2021), Elsie Woolsey in entry for Henry Carver, 1870.

"United States Census, 1880," database with images. *FamilySearch*. https://familysearch.org/ark:/61903/1:1:MFDF-535: 19 February 2021. R M Chambers, Township 13 South Range 67 West, El Paso, Colorado, United States; citing enumeration district ED 45, sheet 469A, NARA microfilm publication T9 (Washington, D.C.: National Archives and Records Administration, n.d.), FHL microfilm 1,254,090.

"United States Census, 1900," database with images. *FamilySearch* https://www.familysearch.org/ark:/61903/1:1:MQMC-436 : 11 March 2022, Robert M Chambers, 1900.

Whorton, James C. *Nature Cures: The History of Alternative Medicine in America.* Oxford: Oxford University Press, 2002. https://search.ebscohost.com/login.aspx?direct=true&db=nlebk&AN=1 20962&site=ehost-li

Wilder, Laura Ingalls. *On the Banks of Plum Creek.* New York: HarperCollins Publishers, 1971.

Wilson, O. Meredith. *The Denver and Rio Grande Project, 1870-1901: A History of the First Thirty Years of the Denver and Rio Grande Railroad.* Salt Lake City: Westwater Press, 1981.

Made in the USA
Coppell, TX
24 March 2023

14686163R00077